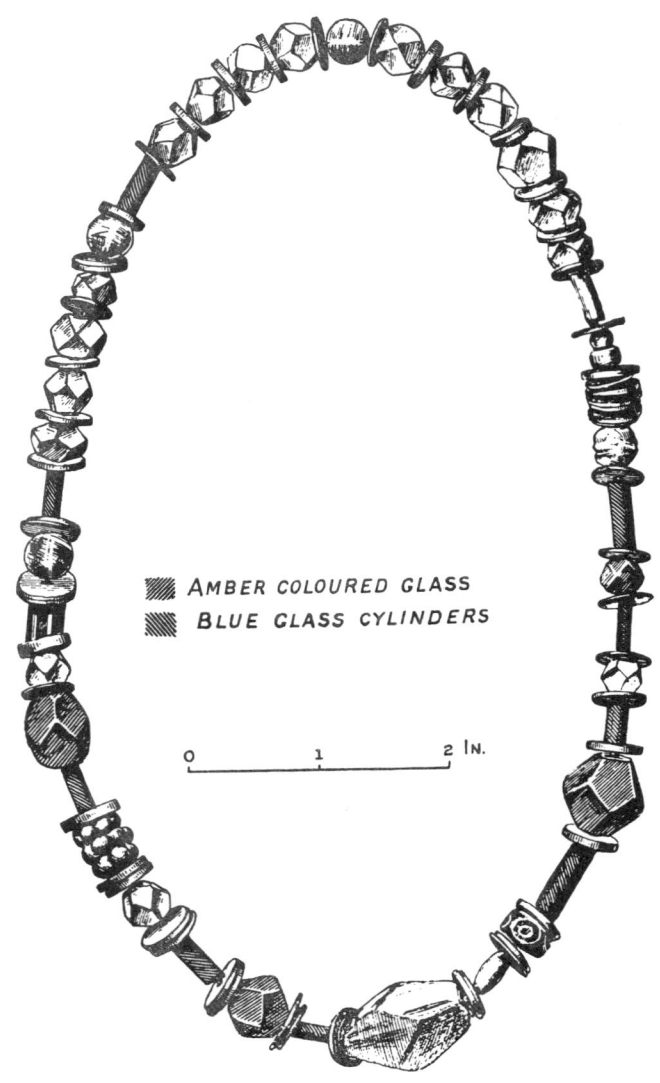

A necklace of Amsterdam beads from west Africa.

A Handbook on Beads

W. G. N. van der SLEEN

GEORGE SHUMWAY PUBLISHER
York * Pennsylvania

DEDICATION

To my wife Marianne

ISBN 0-87387-060-3

GEORGE SHUMWAY PUBLISHER
RD7 Box 388b * YORK * PA. 17402

Table of Contents

	Page
Editorial, by Joseph PHILIPPE	4
LIST OF ILLUSTRATIONS	7
Foreword, by D.B. HARDEN	11
Preface	12

PART ONE
Nomenclature and classification of beads 15

CHAPTER I :
Beads in general 17

CHAPTER II :
Glass 19

CHAPTER III :
The fabrication and technique of glass beads 22

CHAPTER IV :
Glossary of terms used in describing glass beads 29
A. General terms 30
B. Ratio of length of bead to its diameter 33
C. Types of beads, based on Beck's terminology 34
    a. Glossary of terms for standard shapes 35
    b. Glossary of terms for special shapes 38
    c. Some special shapes of beads 41
    d. Glossary of types of ornamented beads 44
    e. Coloured beads 50

CHAPTER V :
Classification of beads 51

PART TWO
What is known about beads and their distribution 53

CHAPTER I :
Prehistoric beads 55

CHAPTER II :
Beads from Mesopotamia 58

CHAPTER III :
Egyptian beads 61

CHAPTER IV :
Phœnician and Punic beads 65

	Pages
CHAPTER V : Beads from Persia	69
CHAPTER VI : Beads from India	73
CHAPTER VII : Beads from the East African coast	76
A. Zanzibar	76
B. Kilwa Kisiwani	87
C. Malindi	88
D. Madagascar	88
E. Sofala	91
CHAPTER VIII : Beads from the Rhodesian ruins	92
CHAPTER IX : Beads from the Indian Ocean and farther east	96
A. Malaya	96
B. Indonesia	98
C. China	102
D. Japan	102
CHAPTER X : Beads from West Africa	103
CHAPTER XI : Ancient beads in Europe	106
CHAPTER XII : Beads from 17th-century Amsterdam	108
CHAPTER XIII : Modern beads	113
A. Venice	113
B. Gablonz	114
C. Kaufbueren	114
D. Briare	114
E. Hebron	115
CHAPTER XIV : Aboriginal modern beads	116
A. Africa	116
B. North America	117
C. South America	119
BIBLIOGRAPHY	120
INDEX	125
TABLE OF CONTENTS	141

List of illustrations

Frontispiece. A necklace of Amsterdam beads from west-Africa.
In Part I. Figs. 3-6 after H.C. BECK.
In Part II. Mostly by Mrs. M.J.A. v. D. SLEEN.

PART I
NOMENCLATURE AND CLASSIFICATION OF BEADS

Fig. 1. How wound glass beads are made (p. 20).
Photograph of multiple-wound short bicones of opaque glass (p. 22).
Fig. 2. How drawn glass beads are made (p. 24).
Fig. 3. Some general terms explained (p. 28).
Fig. 4. Standard types of beads (p. 32).
Fig. 5. Some special shapes of beads (p. 41).
Fig. 6. Some types of ornamented beads (p. 42).

PART II
WHAT IS KNOWN ABOUT BEADS AND THEIR DISTRIBUTION

Colour plate of glass beads and of tubes (pp. 54/55).
PLATE I (p. 60) :
Fig. 1. A prehistoric bead. A horse's front tooth, perforated and with three scratches on the enamel, Solutrean cave near Carsac, Dordogne. About 15000 B.C.
Figs. 2 and 3. Prehistoric types of cornelian beads, used by many civilizations.
  Fig. 2. A short hexagonal truncated bicone from Deir Alla in Jordan, 12th century A.D.
  Fig. 3. A long hexagonal bicone from Celebes, Indonesia, 19th century A.D.
Figs. 4 to 8. Faience beads from Mesopotamia, found in Egypt as well.
  Fig. 4. A reticulated lozenge bead.
  Fig. 5. A reticulated cylindrical bead.
  Fig. 6. A truncated barrel bead, reticulated.
  Fig. 7. A combed ogee bead of very brittle faience. Amlash, Persia.
  Fig. 8. A collared green barrel bead.
Figs. 9 to 13. Faience beads from Egypt.
  Fig. 9. Segmented beads. From Predynastic to Ptolemaic.
  Fig. 10. Mummy-net beads and small spacing beads. 1300 B.C.
  Fig. 11. Raised faience crumb bead. 9th Dynasty.
  Fig. 12. Eye-pendant of black glass with yellow ring.
  Fig. 13. Melon bead. Green or blue faience and blue cobalt glass. Pompeii, Roman.
Figs. 14 and 15.
  Fig. 14. Chequer beads, built up from many slices of rods. 7th to 9th cent. A.D.
  Fig. 15. Chevron bead. Amsterdam or Venice. 15th to 20th cent. A.D.
PLATE II (p. 66) :
Figs. 16 to 19. Glass beads and pendant from Punic Carthage. Nat. size.
  Fig. 16. Phœnician pendant showing the mask of a bearded man. Lavigerie Museum, Carthage. 400-300 B.C.

Fig. 17. Glass bead of large size and large perforation. Opaque blue glass with numerous yellow eyes. Lavigerie Museum, Carthage. 300 B.C.
Fig. 18. Large cigar-shaped opaque brown glass bead with yellow combed lines. Lavigerie Museum, Carthage and Bardo Museum, Tunis. 300 B.C.
Fig. 19. Globular ornamented glass bead, blue and yellow. Lavigerie Museum, Carthage.
Fig. 20. Misformed glass bead, blue with yellow eyes. Tarsus, Cilicia. 300 B.C.
Fig. 21. Eye-bead with black eye in white ring on green glass bead. Persia. 150 B.C.
Fig. 22. Eye-bead with two unequal rows of eyes. Blue on bluish. Persia.
Fig. 23. Stratified eye-bead. Blue and white glass. Persia.
Fig. 24. Glass horned eye-bead with inset pieces of rods. Persia. A.D.

PLATE III (p. 68) :
Figs. 25 to 36. Beads from Persia and India.
Fig. 25. Cornelian tabular bead, etched white. Persia. A B.C. type.
Fig. 26. Cornelian truncated barrel bead etched with lines and dots. Persia. A B.C. type.
Fig. 27. Cornelian tabular bead. Persia. A B.C. type (mostly).
Fig. 28. Cornelian ornamented pendant. Rare form. Persia. Probably a B.C. type.
Fig. 29. Cornelian drop pendant. Persia. Made till now in Cambay.
Fig. 30. Cornelian multifaceted bead. Persia. Probably modern.
Fig. 31. Quartz cornerless cube. Persia. B.C.
Fig. 32. Quartz ornamented bead, green glazed. Persia. B.C.
Fig. 33. Large, dark green, glass cylinder bead, often squared, with yellow-green spots, outlined with red. Persia. First centuries A.D. Found along the old silk route all the way to China and Indonesia.
Fig. 34. Mameluke bead. Ornamented with yellow to green lobes and ogee-forms. In Persia, Jordan, Syria and Egypt. 12th to 15th cent. A.D.
Fig. 35. Syrian bead. Black glass, often deteriorated, with white zones and a zig-zag line. Persia and Jordan. First centuries A.D.?
Fig. 36. Spirally-wound glass beads up to 5 cm. in rainbow-like colours. Interference by disintegration. Persia.

Figs. 37 to 44. Indian beads, mostly from Kausambi near Allahabad. 200 B.C. - A.D. 200.
Fig. 37. Etched cornelian bead. White on orange.
Fig. 38. Black etchings on orange cornelian bead.
Fig. 39. Blacked cornelian bead with white etching.
Fig. 40. Hand-perforated green glass bead. Flattened.
Fig. 41. Spirally wound Indian-red bead.
Fig. 42. Folded blue bead with white lines.

Fig. 43. Black globular bead with red spiral lines.
Fig. 44. Two collared green glass beads, the lower with mosaic inset.

PLATE IV (p. 80) :
Figs. 45 to 48. Ancient beads from Zanzibar. All opaque glass and all made in India.
Fig. 45. Biconical to globular multiple-wound beads. A.D. 400-800.
Fig. 46. Multiple-wound lenticular bead. A.D. 400 to 800.
Numbers 45 and 46 occur in Indian-red, yellow and greenish blue like 47 and 48, but the latter are drawn beads and come into use only about A.D. 800 to 1600. These are the trade-wind beads that were carried by Indians and Arabs all over the Indian Ocean from Sofala to China.
Fig. 47. Short, opaque glass cylinder bead, drawn. Indian-red, yellow and blue-green. Imported by Indians, Arabs and, later, Portuguese.
Fig. 48. Long, opaque, drawn glass cylinder bead in same colours as 45-47.

Figs. 50 to 59. Modern beads from Venice and Gablonz, that took the place of the Indian bead after 1600 in the trade with the Bantu.
Fig. 49. Spirally-wound oval beads of modern colours and shining glass. Probably the first European glass beads that came to east Africa.
Fig. 50. Ox-eye bead. Coated with 1 mm. clear red over a thick white kernel. Drawn.
Fig. 51. Transparent wine red over thin white kernel. 1600 A.D. until today. Trade name in America « cornaline d'Aleppo ».
Fig. 52. Thin opaque red over white or yellow in all sizes.
Fig. 53. Thin Indian red over blue, green or brown glass. Drawn. The spirit bead of the Bantu woman.
Fig. 54. Cornerless hexagonal cylinder of dark blue glass. Cook travelled round the world with these beads.
Fig. 55. Annular or ring beads. Cobalt blue. Worn by the chief who met Livingstone at the Falls, 1856.
Fig. 56. Spotted beads, black with white spots. Palm-oil trade.
Fig. 57. Palm-leaf or feather bead, in use from 1st to 20th cent. A.D.
Fig. 58. Beads with spiral lines of twisted blue and white glass trails.
Fig. 59. Arabesque bead. Used e.g., by Stanley in his search for Livingstone.
Fig. 60. Mosaic bead. Used for the last 200 years in west Africa.
Fig. 61. Millefiori bead. Still welcome in west Africa.

PLATE V (p. 86) :

Figs. 62 to 64 are the so called seed beads, used for beadwork by the Bantu.
Fig. 62 a. Seed beads used before 1910. 5 mm. diameter.
Fig. 62 b. Seed beads after 1910. Size 2 to 3 mm.
Fig. 63. A Bantu love letter in coloured seed beads.
Fig. 64. Part of an intricate collar of seed beads.
Figs. 65 and 66. Shell beads cut out of the large Tridacna shells.
Fig. 67. Mpande or Ndoro, the top of a Conus shell, polished, worth a maiden. Now more cherished in red plastic, but of less value !
Figs. 68 and 69. Porcelain beads, cylinder (drum-like) or bicones, very precise in form, from the French factory at Briare. Congo.
Figs. 70 to 73. Ancient beads from Johore (Gardner collection).
Fig. 70. Combed bead from Johore (Malacca). Yellow rings on black bead.
Fig. 71. Horned eye-bead from Malacca.
Fig. 72. Faience spacing-beads.
Fig. 73. Spiral wound long oval bead. Indian-red.
Photograph of beads from Flores (p. 98).

PLATE VI (p. 101) :

Figs. 74 to 77. Beads from Flores, Indonesia, NOT made in Europe or India.
Fig. 74. Very small ringlets of orange-brown glass, wound and very heavy, containing a high percentage of lead. Called Muti Sala.
Fig. 75. Small oval beads of clear wine-red glass. Wound.
Fig. 76. Globular beads of the same glass. Wound.
Fig. 77. Globular and wound wine-red as before, but pinched into a squarish form.
Figs. 78 to 81. Four types of beads collected on Flores, made in Amsterdam in the 17th century.
Fig. 78. A mulberry bead. Clear, white or dark blue glass.
Fig. 79. Gold-leaf bead. Gold foil between two layers of glass.
Fig. 80. Chevron bead, made of six superimposed layers of coloured glass, greenish, white, blue, red, white and blue.
Fig. 81. Pentagon bead, mostly amber-coloured, but in white and blue as well.

PLATE VII (p. 104):
European beads of Merovingian times. A.D. 450-750. All these beads are wound and hand-decorated except 83, 84 and 97.
Fig. 82. Oblate bead with single wavy line.
Fig. 83. Segmented beads, often in blue or gold-leaf glass.
Fig. 84. Short biconical bead.
Fig. 85. Oval bead with spiral eye decoration.
Fig. 86. Oblate bead with two crossing wavy lines.
Fig. 87. Globular bead with two crossing wavy lines and dots.
Fig. 88. Truncated barrel bead with wide crossing wavy lines.
Fig. 89. Large brown cylinder bead with combed rings of yellow glass.
Fig. 90. Yellow oblate bead with green lobes.
Fig. 91. Large oblate bead zoned with three parallel wavy lines.
Fig. 92. White cylinder bead with pink combed rings.
Fig. 93. Scallop bead.
Fig. 94. Biconical, truncated zigzag bead.
Fig. 95. Red-capped millefiori bead with yellow flowers on green.
Fig. 96. Smooth crumb bead with coloured bits of glass in black.
Fig. 97. Slightly biconical opaque bead of strange colours, such as grey, dark red, dark green, dark blue and orange. After A.D. 600.
Fig. 98. Short cylinder bead with wide crossed wavy lines and eyes in between the waves.
Fig. 99. Single eye-bead with blue pupil in white ring on green bead.
Fig. 100. Biconical black and white zoned bead.

Photographs of Amsterdam beads Nos. 1 and 2 (p. 105).
Photographs of Amsterdam beads Nos. 3 and 4 (p. 106).
Second colour-plate of glass beads (pp. 106/107).
Photograph of pipe and pipe bowls (p. 107).

PLATE VIII (p. 109):
Figs. 101 to 120. Beads made in Amsterdam, 17th century.
  Fig. 101. Rough globular wound bead of milk white, light and dark blue glass.
  Fig. 102. Rough, oval wound bead of milk white, light and dark blue glass.
  Fig. 103. Pentagonal cylinder of milk white, light and dark blue glass.
  Fig. 104. Large pentagon bead, often amber-coloured.
Nos. 101 to 104 are the first products of the Amsterdam factory.
  Fig. 105. Glass tube or cylinder bead, often coloured.
  Fig. 106. Striped cylinder bead, that occurs in many colours.
  Fig. 107. Spirally-striped cylinder bead.
  Fig. 108. Banded cylinder bead.
Nos. 105 to 108 are often broken off irregularly as they are the remains of drawn tubes, which had to be cut to get cylinder beads.
  Figs. 109 to 112. Misformed beads, refuse of the factory.
  Fig. 113. Globular or oblate beads of many colours, wound as well as drawn, in all sizes.
  Fig. 114. Black beads striped with white or yellow. Coloured black by iron.
  Fig. 115. Similar black beads with irregular crossing wavy lines.
  Fig. 116. White long oval bead with triple blue spiral lines.
  Fig. 117. Mulberry bead in clear glass or dark blue.
  Fig. 118. Double cylinder of clear glass with gold leaf in between.
  Fig. 119. Chevron or star or rosette bead mostly of small sizes in Africa, but up to 35 mm. in Amsterdam.
  Fig. 120. Pentagon beads in clear, white, blue and specially in amber-coloured glass, very much used for barter in Indonesia.
Figs. 121 to 124. Beads made from powdered glass by west African natives.
  Fig. 121. Garden-roller bead, made of seed beads, in a mould. South Rhodesia.
  Fig. 122. Beads made of layers of powdered glass from medicine-bottles.
  Fig. 123. Striped beads made of layers of powdered glass from medicine-bottles.
  Fig. 124. Spirally banded beads made of layers of powdered glass from medicine-bottles.

Foreword

The Committee of the J.I.V., anxious that it should take its full part in facilitating publication of research on the history of glass, decided at its meeting in Damascus in November 1964 that the J.I.V. should initiate a series of monographs, to supplement and support its existing series of *Bulletins* and *Annales des Congrès*. The *Bulletins* describe glass-making and glass-collections in individual countries and also contain information about new discoveries and about the activities of J.I.V. itself. The *Annales des Congrès* contain, as their name implies, the proceedings of the (normally triennial) J.I.V. meetings, including shortened versions of the communications read at them by scholars. Each of these series, therefore, has a specific task to fulfil and neither provides a *milieu* for the publication of works of scholarship in general.

Seeking a subject suitable for the first monograph in the new series, the Committee decided that one of the greatest needs, not only for students of glass, but for scholars in general, was an up-to-date handbook on the typology and terminology of beads. Having taken this decision the Committee had no doubt about who should be invited to undertake such a task, for they knew that in Dr. van der Sleen they could find not only a collector and traveller who had gathered and studied beads in almost every country in the world, but also a scholar who was likely to be ready and, indeed, anxious to undertake such a handbook in order to pass on his knowledge to others.

And so it turned out. Dr. van der Sleen accepted the Committee's invitation, and it is my pleasant duty, here, to introduce to the public Dr. van der Sleen's book as the first in what we must all hope will be a long series of J.I.V. monographs on aspects of the history of glass.

The Committee wishes to express its deep sense of gratitude to Dr. van der Sleen not only for accepting their invitation but also for the care and attention which he has given to this work; all the more so since in the later stages of preparing the typescript and putting the work through press, Dr. van der Sleen, to our deep regret, underwent a serious illness. They are very sensible of the honour he has done them in permitting their new series to be the medium through which his work — the fruits of many years of study — is presented to the public and they are happy to commend his book to students of glass and of beads in all lands.

D.B. HARDEN,
President.

Preface

Definition of « Beads » given in the *ENCYCLOPAEDIA BRITANNICA* (1938), vol. III, p. 251 :
« A bead is a small globule or ball, used in necklaces, etc., and made of a great variety of materials. »
This seems to be too narrow.
On p. 252 there is another attempt :
« A bead is any pierced object, that might be strung ».
This seems to be too wide.
In the 1964 edition there is no definition.

It was midnight on New Years eve of 1954. My wife and I stood on top of a hill in the South African bush. The Reverend Mr. S. of the Swedish Missionpost of Masingo in Southern Rhodesia, not far from the famous ruins of Zimbabwe, had asked us to ring in the New Year for him, as he and his wife were tired after celebrating Christmas with their black flock.

It was a dark and stormy night and strong gusts of rain and wind howled around the belfry. Thunder and lightning filled the sky and over and over again the fierce light showed the mountain tops around us and the small huts of the Bantu, hardly visible through the rain. Here and there, as aroused by the vibrating sounds of the bells, a small red light showed up for a few seconds. We stood as if paralysed by the magnificence of this wild play of the forces of nature and then and there – were they really white straight lines on the flat top of yonder hill ? Another extra fierce flash of lightning left no doubt : there must be something – not nature's work on that hill ! We marked the direction with the help of the four feet of the heavy clock-tower and went down, home to the rondavel, which the kind missionaries had put at our disposal.

Of course our next day's picnic brought us up to the other hill. What would it be ? A geological outcrop, walls, just rows of stone or ruins ? They were indeed ruins, foundations of well-cut stone work. We soon found the heap of ash and refuse, that is easiest to analyse without much digging, and there they were, bones and stones, potsherds, some pieces of iron and bronze and ... beads. Tiny glass beads, smaller than 3 mm., red and yellow and blue or green. By sieving I gathered a few hundred and when I had strung them nicely, it struck me at once what the difference was between these old beads and those which the Bantu wear now. All my beads were opaque and there was not a white one amongst them. The necklaces and armlets of today all shine in much brighter colours and are mostly transparent.

I was interested to know how old these glass beads could be and where they came from. The museums in Salisbury and Bulawayo, Elisabethville, Pretoria, Durban, Grahamstown, Capetown, etc., had a few « ruin » beads, but nobody could tell me where they came from. We travelled on and I collected hundreds of them on the Island of Zanzibar, where they have thousands in the museum. On to London, Paris, Brussels, Amsterdam, Venice, of course, and elsewhere. My beads were practically unknown in Europe : they certainly did not come from Egypt. Interest grew, till at last I met them in literature from India. I travelled on to Calcutta, Jaipur, Allahabad, etc., and there I found the « ruin » beads and the factories where they had been made.

In the meantime I had come to the conclusion that these beads could be found all around the Indian Ocean, just so far as the monsoons or trade-winds blow. That is why I introduced them to the world as trade-wind beads ([1]). These beads, whether they came from Zimbabwe or Zanzibar, Madagascar or Java, were so much alike in technique and colour and form, that you could hardly doubt their identity. But still, proof was only possible by chemical analyses. Now chemical analysing of glass is an extremely difficult and painstaking work, that can only be done in a few specialized laboratories. Happily I found Dr. Vittorio Gottardi and Miss M. Tornati able and willing to undertake the difficult, tedious job, working as they were in the new Stazione Sperimentale del Vetro in Murano. The result of these analyses ([2]) proved more than we had hoped for. Not only could the identity of the trade-wind beads from Zanzibar with the Indian beads be proved, but all the Indian beads showed a certain amount, up to 5 %, of phosphoric acid compounds, which had never been found before in ancient beads.

([1]) van der SLEEN, W.G.N., 1956, « Trade-wind beads », *Man*, n⁰ 27.
([2]) TORNATI, Maria, and van der SLEEN, 1960, « L'analisi chimica aiuta l'archeologia », *Vetro e silicati*, IV, n⁰ 23.

The reader will understand that this long search for the origin of the trade-wind beads over three large continents deepened both my interest in, and my knowledge of beads. On all these trips I met many people who were interested in old glass and even a few who were interested in glass beads. They all felt and expressed the need of a Handbook where the few things known about this material were collected, and that is why I began the writing of this book.

Inevitably the following chapters must be very incomplete. Much has been written on beads in languages such as Russian, Polish, Japanese, etc., which few west European people can read and understand. At the same time many important publications are printed in magazines and periodicals that appear only in very small editions. Still worse, many excavation-reports are never printed at all, or tell us no more than the number of beads found on a particular site.

That I still risk this publication, knowing very well that it falls far short of what it should be, happens in the hope that more archaeologists will pay more attention to beads and that many of them will be kind enough to send me offprints of their publications or at least references to them.

Happily I have travelled much over three-quarters of our civilized world and in some uncivilized parts as well. So I can depend much on my own collection and on a great deal of material that has been sent to me for identification.

*
* *

My sincere thanks are extended to many archaeological workers, specially Dr. D.B. Harden, Dir. of the London Museum; Dr. Joseph Philippe, Dir. du Musée du Verre at Liège; Miss G. Caton Thompson of Broadway, Worcestershire; M. Jean Beguin, Liège; Dr. G. Fingerlin, Freiburg, Germany; Dott. Michelangelo Pasquato, Venice; Prof. Dr. M. G. Dikshit, Univ. of Nagpur, India; Prof. M. Millot, Musée de l'Homme, Paris; Dr. Paul N. Perrot, Corning Museum of Glass, Corning, N. Y.; Dr. Vittorio Gottardi, Stazione Sperimentale del Vetro, Murano; Mr. K.E. Kidd, Royal Ontario Museum, Toronto; Dr. P. Pratt, Fort Stanwix Museum, Rome, N. Y.; Miss Winkler, c/o Hagemeyer, Amsterdam; Mrs. G. Beck, Salisbury, Wiltshire; Dr. Maria Dekowna, Warsaw; and Mr. R.J. Charleston, Victoria and Albert Museum, London.

PART ONE

Nomenclature and Classification of Beads

On 19th October 1926 Horace C. Beck read a paper to the Society of Antiquaries of London entitled « Classification and Nomenclature of Beads and Pendants », which was printed two years later ([1]). He ends his introduction on page 1 with the words : « To describe a bead fully, it is necessary to state its form, perforation, colour, material and decoration ». According to today's knowledge this is not enough.

One of the first things to be known about a bead is how it has been manufactured, as this may be one of the first points to consider when we try to find out when it was made and used ([2]).

Except for this omission, Beck's classification is so complete and logical that I can certainly do no better than adopt it. After that we must first agree internationally on a glossary in at least six languages covering the most common forms of beads and then see what possibility there is of dating beads by other finds and dating other finds by the beads that have been found in the same tomb or stratum. This glossary will not only be useful for glass beads but also for beads of stone, mineral, ivory and other materials. With glass beads, knowledge of the chemical composition of the glass may also be of great importance. Large quantities of lead, for instance, will be a very interesting phenomenon, just as will small quantities of phosphorus or molybdenum ([3]).

---

[1] BECK, H.C. (1928), « Classification and nomenclature of beads and pendants », *Archaeologia*, LXXVII, pp. 1-76.
[2] van der SLEEN, W.G.N. (1958), « Ancient glass beads from east and central Africa and the Indian Ocean », *J. Roy. Anthrop. Inst.*, LXXXVIII, pt. II.
[3] CALVI, M.C., *Roman Glass at Aquileia* (forthcoming).

CHAPTER I

Beads in general

I think we can say that beads are older than civilization. Shells, teeth, seeds, etc., could easily be pierced and strung into necklaces and bracelets. Small bits of stalactites, alternating with dog-teeth, will have looked nice on a brown skin. The bow-drill is nearly as old as civilization and ornamental stones like agate could be pierced and strung long before the pyramids were built. Three thousand years before Christ amethyst, cornelian and garnet were ground, polished and pierced. This was done in Egypt as well as in Mesopotamia, where, specially, lapis lazuli was worked into globular and cylindrical beads, that probably came as barter to predynastic Egypt. In the same period we find man-made beads of baked sand with a small addition of some loam or lime which has been given the name of frit or faience. In frit the sand grains adhere so loosely that you may scrape them away with your finger-nail.

In faience there is much more adhesion between the particles so that, on a fractured edge, the core may look like porcelain (china) or, better, earthenware. These beads could be « glazed », as we call it, by covering their surface with alkali in a coloured solution before the baking is done. This « faience » was still used in Ptolemaic and Roman times, in Egypt as well as in Mesopotamia and Persia.

While in glass beads the perforation is a natural result of the methods of manufacture, stone beads must be perforated by drilling. This drilling or boring was always a dangerous job. Very often, before small steel drills could be used, the pressure on the drill would cause a segment of the bead to break off. To avoid this in the old days perforation was always begun from both sides, which often made the parts of the channel meet at an angle. This may be seen in transparent beads, but it can always be felt wich a pin, sliding along the wall of the perforation. In this way the best glass imitations of semi-precious stones may be recognized for what they are. I do not yet know when drilling with adequate stell drills began.

o
o o

It is interesting to record that a factory making cornelian, quartz and other stone beads has been working in Cambay, Gujerat, for at least 7000 years and is still active ([1]).

([1]) ARKELL, A.J. (1936), « Cambay and the bead trade », *Antiquity*, X, 292.

CHAPTER II

Glass

The origin or, if you like, the inventor of glass is unknown. I think there is a simple explanation of how it arose.

Faience is made from powdered quartz or quartz-sand, to which a small amount of clay or marl, perhaps some limestone or alkali, is added, to make the mixture cohere when heated. The beads may be formed of this powdery paste around little sticks, placed in hollows in a block of clay. After heating slightly a solution of glaze (soda, potash or nitre) is applied to the surface of the beads and then the block of clay is fired. The little sticks are burned and leave a hole, the perforation of the bead. The alkali unites with the sand of the bead and if a little copper or iron was added to the solution, a beautifully coloured, glazed, shiny faience bead is the result.

Glass is made from the same constituents by melting quartz or quartz-sand with soda, potash or nitre with a little lime and some lead or copper. Faience only differs from glass in having a much smaller amount of alkali. You may try it yourself. Take one of these small faience, tubular beads, that form the nets which covered the mummy-cases of the 18th to the 22nd Dynasties. These are green or blue outside, but inside the break is white. This is not so on all of them. Several tubes will be coloured all through, at least at one end. There they become semi-transparent and are, in fact, just glass, and, if you heat one of these faience beads with a little surplus of soda, it will change into glass. One of the artisans must have observed this, or else he dropped a bit of glaze and saw how it hardened into glass on the floor. From this simple observation the fabrication of real glass must have sprung.

The first glass-makers must have been struck by the close resemblance of some of their products to ornamental stones and we find them from the beginning imitating these products of nature, especially lapis lazuli, onyx and cornelian. The student or collector may be sometimes in doubt in deciding the difference and can be helped, for example, by the fact that glass often contains air-bubbles, or by differences in the perforation, which is always straight in glass beads and is often a broken line in stone beads, which often have been drilled from both sides.

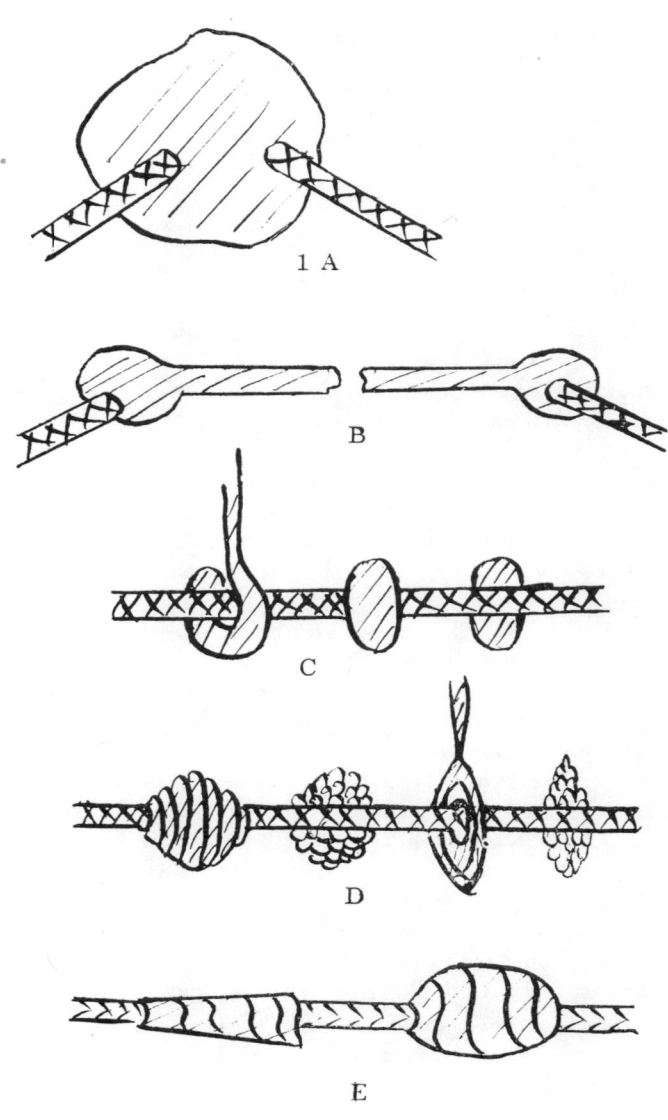

Fig. 1
How WOUND beads are made.

But who were these first glass-makers ? Most archaeologists have for long thought that glass was first made in Egypt, where Flinders Petrie discovered glass workshops, lots of very well made beads and other glass objects. A few years ago, however, we found out that glass-making was flourishing over 200 years earlier under Amenophis I and that the glass-works of Amenophis III could be found at Thebes. This pharaoh's son was the man who tried to do away with all the old Egyptian gods and called himself Akhenaten, Blessed of the Sun-God. It was at his new capital, Tell el Amarna, that Petrie found the first glass-works, that must have been thriving around 1365 B.C. Amenophis I died about 1535 B.C.

Now it is well known, that under these pharaohs Egypt pushed its frontiers farther and farther to the north-east and exchanged presents with the Hittites and other peoples from Babylonia and Assyria. The mother of Akhenaten was said to be a Hittite princess.

Why do I make this excursion into old Egyptian history ? Simply because at the Archaeological Congress of 1965 in Warsaw I met Mrs. Ugrelidza, who handed me her booklet *Glass of Old Georgia from the Third Millennium B.C.* Unfortunately it is written in the Georgian language and printed in old Georgian characters, but those of us who do not understand Georgian can turn to an article by Prof. Bezborodov in *Slavia Antiqua*, 1965, « Early stages in glass-making in U.S.S.R. ». He tells us that glass and beads were made in Russia, just south of the Caucasian Mountains in Georgia, Armenia, Azerbaijan and Tashkent about a thousand years before Tell el Amarna was founded. We must take it as very probable that among the presents sent by the rulers bordering on Egypt were glass objects and glass-workers. Thus the glass-works of Akhenaten were not the beginning of a new period, but the full grown mastery of this art, developed from trials and errors during eight or ten centuries.

CHAPTER III

The fabrication and technique of glass beads

Glass is made in thick earthenware crucibles, which may contain from 2 to 200 pounds of a mixture of pulverized quartz or quartz-sand with alkali (soda, potash or nitre, sometimes even lead) and some lime. The container is heated till the contents consist of red-hot molten glass. Generally, before heating, iron or copper, manganese or cobalt is added to colour the glass. All this must be thoroughly mixed and then melted into a thick, syrupy mass of red-hot, viscous glass. A workman stirs

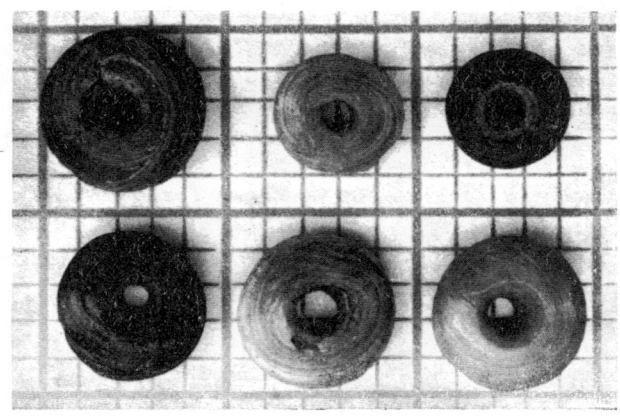

Multiple wound short bicones of opaque glass. Old beads of the 1st millennium A.D., made in India and collected at Zanzibar.
(Photograph by the author.)

this with an iron bar, on the end of which he gathers a lump of melted glass, in which he inserts a second iron bar (fig. 1 A) and hands that bar to another workman, who walks away with it, pulling out the viscous mass to a shiny glass rod (fig. 1 B) that solidifies before it touches the floor. The faster this man goes the thinner the rod will be. It may be pulled out to 100 m. or more and vary in diameter from twelve mm. to one millimetre. These long rods are then cut down to handy lengths of 60 or 90 cm. to become the raw material for making the oldest and simplest kind of beads, the so-called « wound beads ».

WOUND BEADS

Nowadays such glass rods are taken from the glass factory at Murano, for instance, to home-workers in Venice, where ten to twenty girls sit in a room at a large table, each in front of a glass-blowing lamp (blow-torch), their faces protected by a glass plate. They melt one of the glass rods at one end and fold it round a copper or iron wire, which they hold in the other hand. When the glass ring is closed round the wire (fig. 1 C), the rest of the rod is cut off and the wire with the glass ring is turned and heated till the ring is nicely round or oval. When three or five rings have been turned around the wire it is laid aside to cool. In cooling the metal contracts more than the glass and the beads can be stripped off. According to the diameter of the wire we get a wide or narrow perforation. When the wire tapers, the perforation will taper too, which often happened in the old days. Then, too, the heat was often not strong enough to melt a thick rod of glass and larger beads could only be made by winding a rod of 1 or 2 mm. diameter several times around the tapering wire or other core. We must, therefore, emphasize a division between simple wound and multiple wound beads (fig. 1 D). The latter will in several places be the oldest glass beads known.

The reader will easily understand that this way of making beads is a very tedious one as every single bead must be made singly by hand. Most ornamented beads, which we will treat later, are made thus singly by hand. But a much more mechanical method, that gave us the « drawn bead », was later discovered, and beads have been made by this newer process since the beginning of our era. And it is not only the simple globular or oval bead, that can be «drawn». Drawn beads may when still hot, easily be modelled into barrels or cubes or cylinders, prisms, etc., by pressing them with metal objects or by using small moulds, for instance of melon-bead form, fastened on the end of pincers, as has already been described and figured by Antonio Neri (1612) in his *L'Arte Vetraria*.

DRAWN BEADS

Before the lump of red-hot glass is taken out of the furnace with an iron bar, it must have been decided whether drawn or wound beads are

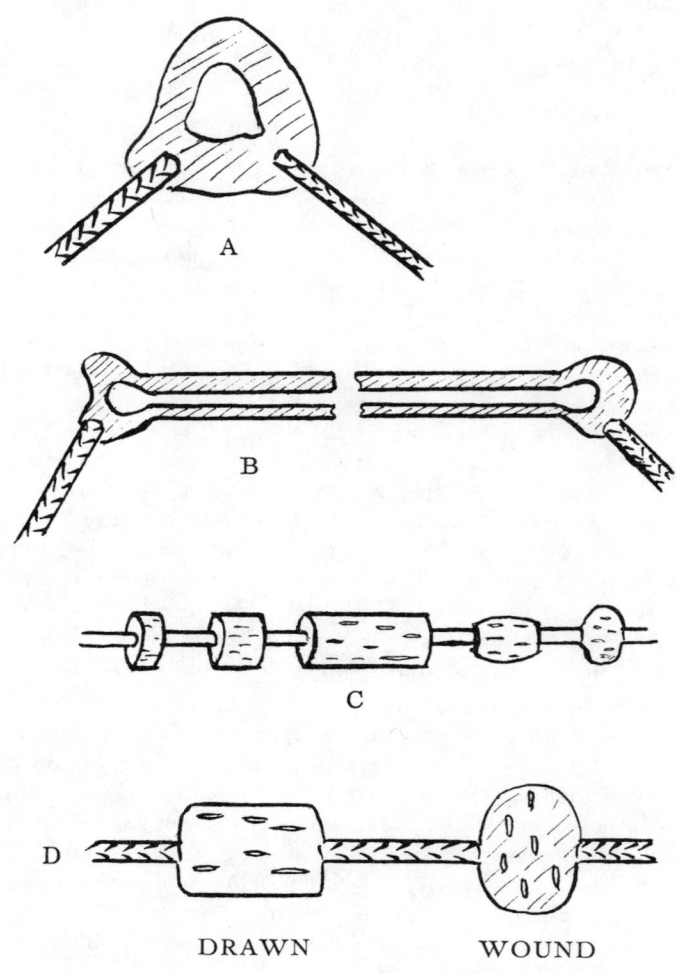

Fig. 2
How DRAWN beads are made.

to be made. To make drawn beads the man who took the glass on his bar will take another bit of iron and work the lump of red-hot glass into a sort of funnel, which he then closes again, so that a large air-bubble is included in the glass (fig. 2 A). Then the second iron bar is taken away again by the second man and now it is not a glass *rod* that comes into existence but a great length of glass *tube* (fig. 2 B). This long tube is out or broken into 90 cm. lengths and a bundle of these tubes is chopped into pieces of 3 mm. or 12 mm., each little piece being a small cylindrical tube, that may be called a bead (fig. 2 C). Of course the process is not so simple as I describe it, but it can be readily understood that each tube, however long it is, will be reduced in a few minutes to perfect beads. Perfect ? Well, the sharp corners must be polished off, but this, too, can be done mechanically, tens of thousands in one revolving barrel. In the bead-trade most of the drawn beads are called « pound beads », as they are generally sold by weight and not by number. These beads are often ground with sharp sand in tumbling-machines that turn them from real cylinders into oblates and even globular beads.

Drawn beads can be ornamented, too, with very few manipulations. We find, for instance, red beads with a white core. To make these the hot bulb of white glass in which an air-filled cavity has already been formed, is rolled over a marble plate to smooth (marver) it. Then it is rolled over a plate of half-molten red glass which sticks to it and when the mass is drawn out, a red bead with a white core is the result, a bead thought so beautiful by many natives that only one tea-spoonful of these small beads was taken as payment for a full day's work in about 1900.

The same result may be reached by dipping the hollow bulb of white glass in a crucible containing molten red glass, that will gather around the white glass so that a tube, drawn out from the bulb, will show the same result, viz. red on white glass, that can be cut down to red on white beads.

Another way of ornamenting drawn beads is to lay differently-coloured strips of glass over the air-filled bulb of glass before drawing out begins. This produces the striped beads that are so often seen. In the first few centuries of our era globular beads were pinched off from the viscous tube of glass with a pair of pincers, resembling those used to make ice-cream balls, but much smaller. In this way segmented beads were made in a long row. These would be broken or sawn into single beads, but often two or three beads were left together. We find this form in the Roman gold-leaf beads and in a blue variety too. Many of the well-known Roman blue melon beads have been made this way.

These kinds of beads are sometimes wrongly called moulded beads, but in glass terminology moulded objects are blown into a form or mould, which I do not think was ever done with such small objects as beads.

Sometimes as many as six layers of different coloured glass are wound around the hollow glass bulb and when the mass thus formed is drawn out and ground and polished chevron beads (rosette or star beads) will be the result.

Some people talk and write about cane beads, meaning cylindrical tube-beads, but a cane is a stick or rod and can never be cut into tubular beads. There are however, a few other methods of bead fabrication which we have to consider, namely folded, pressed, spiral, blown and hand-perforated beads.

FOLDED BEADS

These are made from flattened rods of glass, folded around a wire, in the same way as the wound beads. Often the line where the ends were melted together is clearly visible, running parallel to the perforation. These beads were rather common in the first centuries of our era in India and, sometimes, in Egypt.

PRESSED BEADS

While still half molten, beads of all forms can easily be pressed, e.g. into hexagonal or square beads or even into bicones or barrels with flattened ends. Nowadays many beads are made by pressing the pulverized material into lozenges or tablets like aspirin and then heating them to become porcelain or plastic beads.

SPIRAL BEADS

In Egyptian and Roman times beads were sometimes made by winding thin half-molten rods spirally around a wire, the result being something like a Turritella-shell or a horn of plenty (fig. 1E). They can also be modelled into trigonal or square prisms.

BLOWN BEADS

It is possible to heat part of a glass tube and blow it up to an ellipsoid bead. This method, amongst others, was used for making hollow beads, where gold dust or silver dust was blown in. Nowadays you meet with imitation pearls made thus.

HAND-PERFORATED BEADS

These are made in a great part of India as home-industries. Drops from a molten rod of glass on a soft earthenware dish are perforated with the aid of a hot iron nail, while still plastic.

« BAKED » BEADS OF PULVERIZED GLASS

There are two more ways of making beads that are still practised in west Africa. We can best call them baked beads.

These are made by the aborigines in west Africa from pulverized glass bottles (medicine-bottles). The powder is available in the common three colours, colourless or « white », blue and brown, although I am told that nowadays you can buy the powder in any colour you wish in small plastic bags on the market. The method is the same as was used in ancient Egypt to make faience beads. Holes are made in a lump of clay by pushing in sticks of a quarter of an inch diameter to a depth of about half an inch. A smaller stick the width of a match is placed in the middle of these little holes and then pulverized glass of different colours is inserted in the holes in horizontal layers. When the block of clay is baked in an open fire, the small sticks burn and leave an opening, the perforation of the bead.

The second method is to drop the powder very carefully into a boat-like small hollow stick. In this way interesting striped beads may be made.

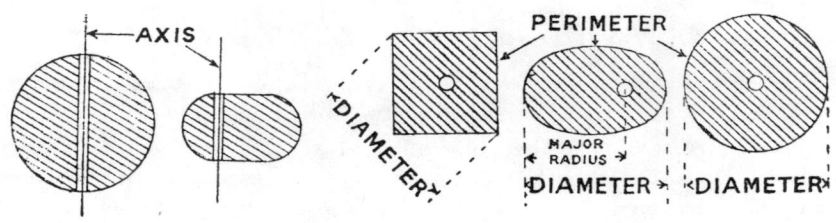

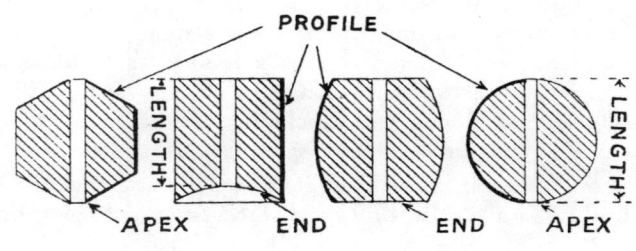

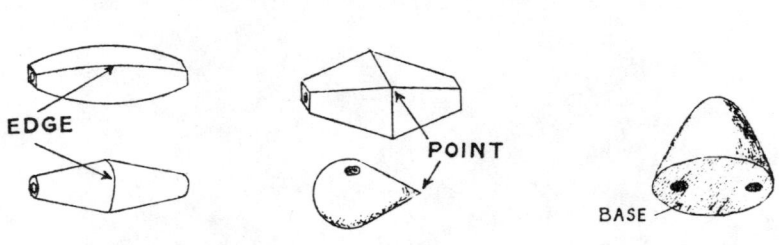

Fig. 3

Some general terms explained.

CHAPTER IV

Glossary of terms used in describing glass beads

U p to now I have been using several terms that are always used in describing beads, but they need to be made very clear and understandable. I have tried, therefore, to put together a glossary defining all the terms regularly used in describing beads in as many languages as possible. Simple drawings (cf. fig. 3) can often assist us, but there are some terms for which a translation in different languages will be sufficient. This first attempt will of course be incomplete and covers only six languages, English, French, German, Italian, Dutch and Polish. I am sorry that we must leave out Russian and Chinese, because of printing difficulties.

N.B. In archaeological literature the word paste is often incorrectly used, generally to designate opaque glass. Eisen pointed this out and stressed the fact that the term should only be used for objects formed of a plastic material in a cool state.

A. GENERAL TERMS

English	Français	Deutsch
bead	perle	Glasperle
glass	verre	Glas
clear	clair	klar
milky-white	blanc de lait	milchweiss
transparent	transparent	durchsichtig
translucent	translucide	durchscheinend
opaque	opaque	undurchsichtig
black	noir	schwarz
grey	gris	grau
red	rouge	rot
orange	orange	oranienfarbig
yellow	jaune	gelb
green	vert	grün
blue	bleu	blau
indigo	indigo	indigo
violet	violet	violett
white	blanc	weiss
colourless	incolore	farblos
axis	axe	Achse
perforation	perforation	Durchbohrung
diameter	diamètre	Durchmesser
perimeter	périmètre	Umfang
apex	sommet	Spitze
end	bout	Ende
length	longueur	Länge
base	base	Basis
point	pointe	Punkt
edge	arête, angle	Ecke

Italiano	Nederlands	Polski
perla	kraal	paciorek
vetro	glas	szkło, szklany
limpido	helder	jasny
bianco latte	melkwit	mleczny
trasparante	doorzichtig	przezroczysty
traslucido	doorschijnend	przeświecający (półprzezroczysty)
opaco	ondoorzichtig	nieprzezroczysty
nero	zwart	czarny
grigio	grijs	szary
rosso	rood	czerwony
arancio	oranje	pomarańczowy
giallo	geel	żółty
verde	groen	zielony
azzurro	blauw	niebieski
indigo	indigo	błękitny
violetto	violet	fioletowy
bianco	wit	biały
—	kleurloos	—
asse	as	oś
perforazione	perforatie	przedziurawienie
diametro	diameter	średnica
perimetro	omtrek	obwód
apice	top	wierzchołek
estremità	einde	koniec
lunghezzà	lengte	długośč
base	basis	podstawa
punta	punt	punkt
margine	hoek, kant	krawędź (grań), róg

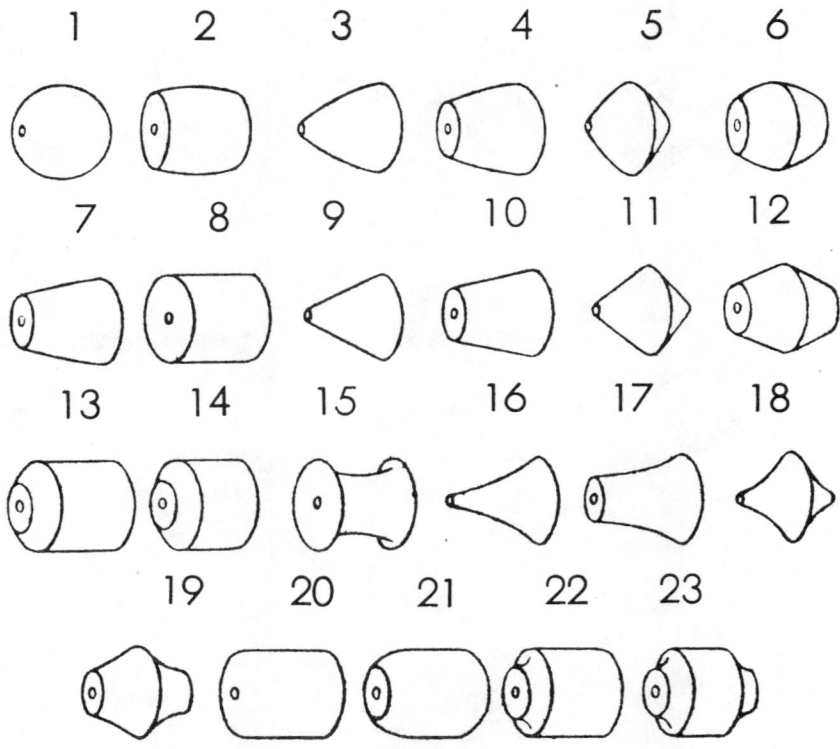

Fig. 4

Standard types of beads, based on Beck's terminology. Beck (1928) gives drawings of the long, short and disc beads as well, but these can easily be understood from the descriptions on p. 33.

B. RATIO OF LENGTH OF BEAD TO ITS DIAMETER

We call a bead standard, when the length is equal to the diameter.

When the length is greater than the diameter, we call it a long bead, when it is less than the diameter it is called a short bead and when it is not more than one third of the diameter it is a disc bead.

Here follow the words used for these terms in our six languages :

English	Français	Deutsch
standard	normale	normal
long	longue	lang
short	courte	kurz
disc	discoïde	scheibenförmig

Italiano	Nederlands	Polski
normale	standaard	normalny
lungo	lang	dlugi
corto	kort	krótki
disco	schijfvormig	tarczowaty

C. TYPES OF BEADS, BASED ON BECK'S TERMINOLOGY
a. *Glossary of terms for standard shapes* (fig. 4, p. 32)

English	Français	Deutsch
1 globular	sphérique	kugelig
2 barrel	en forme de tonneau	tonnenförmig
3 convex cone	conique convexe	konvex-konisch abgestumpft
4 truncated convex cone	tronconique convexe	konvex konisch
5 convex bicone	biconique convexe	konvex doppelkonisch abgestumpft
6 truncated convex bicone	bitronconique convexe	doppelkonisch
7 pear-shaped	piriforme	birnenförmig
8 cylinder	cylindrique	cylindrisch
9 cone	conique	kugelförmig
10 truncated cone	tronconique convexe	abgestumpft konisch
11 bicone	biconique	doppeltkugel
12 truncated bicone	bitronconique	abgestumpft doppelkonisch
13 chamfered cylinder	cylindrique avec une extrémité chanfreinée	abgefast cylindrisch
14 double chamfered cylinder	cylindrique avec deux extrémités chanfreinées	zweiseitig abgefast cylindrisch
15 concave cylinder	cylindrique concave	spulenförmig
16 concave cone	conique concave	konkav konisch
17 truncated concave cone	tronconique concave	abgestumpft konkav konisch
18 concave bicone	biconique concave	konkav doppelkonisch

Italiano	Nederlands	Polski
1 sferico	bolvormig	kulisty
2 a barile	tonvormig	beczułkowaty
3 cono convesso	convexe kegel	w kształcie wypukłego stożka
4 cono troncato convesso	geknot convexe kegel	w kształcie ściętego wypukłego stożka
5 bicono convesso	convexe dubbel kegel	w kształcie dwóch złączonych podstawami wypukłych stożków
6 bicono troncato convesso	geknotte dubbel kegel	w kształcie dwóch złączonych podstawami ściętych wypukłych stożków
7 forma di pera	peervormig	gruszkowaty
8 cylindrico	cylinder	cylindryczny
9 conico	kegelvormig	stożkowaty
10 cono troncato	geknot kegelvormig	w kształcie ściętego stożka
11 bicono	dubbelkegel	dwustożkowaty
12 bicono troncato	geknotte dubbelkegel	w kształcie dwóch złączonych podstawami ściętych stożków
13 cilindro con una estremità smussata	afgeschuinde cylinder	cylindryczny ze ściętymi krawędziami na jednymi końcu
14 cilindro con ambedue estremita smussate	dubbel afgeschuinde cylinder	cylindryczny ze ściętymi krawędziami na obu końcach
15 cilindro concavo	concave cylinder	szpulowaty
16 cono concavo	concave kegel	w kształcie wklęsłego stożka
17 cono concavo troncato	geknotte concave kegel	w kształcie ściętego wklęsłego stożka
18 bicono concavo	geknotte dubbelkegel	w kształcie dwóch złączonych podstawami wklęsłych stożków

English	Français	Deutsch
19 truncated concave bicone	bitronconique concave	abgestumpft konkav doppelkonisch
20 cylinder with one convex end	cylindrique avec une extrémité convexe	cylindrisch mit einem abgerundeten ende
21 cylinder with two convex ends	cylindrique avec deux extrémités convexes	cylindrisch mit zwei abgerundeten enden
22 cylinder with one concave end	cylindrique avec une extrémité concave	cylindrisch mit einem gekehlten ende
23 cylinder with two concave ends	cylindrique avec deux extrémités concaves	cylindrisch mit gekehlten enden

Italiano	Nederlands	Polski
19 bicono concavo troncato	geknotte concave dubbelkegel	w kształcie dwóch złączonych podstawami ściętych wklęsłych stożków
20 cilindro con una estremità convessa	cylinder met één convex einde	cylindryczny z zaokrąglonym jednym końcem
21 cilindro con due estremita convesse	cylinder met twee convexe einden	cylindryczny z zaokrąglonymi dwoma końcam
22 cilindro con una estremità concava	cylinder met concaaf einde	cylindryczny z wklęsło ściętym jednym końcem
23 cilindro con due estremita concave	cylinder met twee concave uiteinden	cylindryczny z wklęsło ściętymi obu końcami

b. *Glossary of terms for special shapes* (fig. 5, p. 41)

	English	Français	Deutsch
1	oblate	sphérique, aplati(e) aux bouts	kugelig mit abgeplattenen Enden
2	oval or ellipsoid	ovale ou ellipsoïdal(e)	oval oder elliptisch
3	annular	annulaire	ringförmig
4	tabular	tabulaire	tafelförmig
5	lenticular	lenticulaire	linsenförmig
6	trigonal prism	prismatique triangulaire	dreikantiger Zylinder
7	cube	cubique	würfelförmig
8	rectangular prism	prismatique quadrangulaire	vierkantiger Zylinder
9	pentagonal prism	prismatique pentagonal	fünfkantiger Zylinder
10	hexagonal prism	prismatique hexagonal	sechskantiger Zylinder
11	cornerless cube	cubique aux coins coupés	würfel mit abgeschrägten Ecken
12	cornerless octogonal prism	prismatique octogonal aux coins coupés	8-kantiger Zylinder mit abgeschrägten Ecken
13	lozenge-form	losangique	rautenförmig
14	collared bead	perle à collier	Perle mit kragen
15	capped bead	perle à chappe polaire	kugelig mit gekappten Enden
16	segmented bead	perle segmentée	Segmentperle
17	lozenge faceted	facetté(e) losangique	rautenförmig fazettiert
18	multi-faceted	à facettes multiples	vielfach fazettiert
19	melon-bead	perles à côtes de melon	Melonenperle
20	fluted bead	perle cannelée	konkav gerippt
21	mulberry or raspberry	perle en forme de mûre ou de framboise	himbeerförmig
22	horizontal spacing bead	perle à percements horizontaux	horizontale Schieberperle
23	vertical spacing bead	perle à percements verticaux	verticale Schieberperle
24	double spacing bead	perle à double percements	doppelte Verteilerperle
25	pentagon bead	perles à facettes pentagonales	Perle mit pentagonalen Fazetten

Italiano	Nederlands	Polski
1 sferoidale, compresso ai poli	afgeplatte bol	kulisty, ze spłaszczonymi końcami
2 ovale oppura elissoide	ovaal of ellipsoid	owalny lub elipsoidalny
3 anulare	ringvormig	pierścieniowaty
4 apiattito	geplet a.d. perforatie	silnie spłaszczony
5 lenticulare	lensvormig	soczewkowaty
6 cilindro triangolare	driehoekige cylinder	trójboczny cylindryczny
7 cubo	kubus	w kształcie sześcianu
8 cilindro rettangulare	rechthoekige cylinder	czteroboczny cylindryczny
9 cilindro pentagonale	vijfhoekige cylinder	pięcioboczny cylindryczny
10 cilindro esagonale	zeshoekige cylinder	sześcioboczny cylindryczny
11 cubo senza angoli	kubus met afgeslepen hoeken	w kształcie sześcianu ze ściętymi rogami
12 cilindro ottagonale a angoli smussati	8-hoekige cylinder met afgeslepen hoeken	ośmioboczny cylindryczny ze ściętymi rogami
13 a losanga	ruitvormig	romboidalny
14 a collare	gekraagde kraal	paciorek z kołnierzykowatymi częściami przyotworowymi
15 perla a poli uncappucciati	bol met polaire kappen	paciorek z nakładkami na końcach
16 perle segmentate	gesegmenteerde kraal	paciorek segmentowy
17 pcrla a losanga sfacettati	ruitvormig gefacetteerd	rombowato facetowany
18 perla a sfaccettatura molte plice	veelvuldig gefacetteerd	wielokrotnie facetowany
19 perla a melone	meloenkraal	paciorek melonowaty
20 perla scanalata	concaaf geribd	paciored kanelurowany
21 perla a mura, a lampone	moerbeikraal	morwowaty lub malinowaty
22 perla a distribuire orizzontale	horizontale verdeelkraal	paciorek wieloczęściowy z poziomym podziałem
23 perla a distribuire verticale	verticale verdeelkraal	paciored wieloczęściowy z pionowym podziałem
24 perla a distribuire duplo	dubbele verdeelkraal	paciorek dwuczęściowy
25 perla con facette pentagonale	vijfhoekkraal	paciorek z pięciokątnymi ściankami

I hope that these lists (*a* and *b*), in conjunction with figures 4 and 5, will enable the reader to select the descriptive name for any particular bead, but I want to add remarks on the following items in list *b* :

N° 1, the oblate, has the same shape as the earth. Is it not strange that most European languages have no special name for this form ? N° 4, the tabular bead, has two flat sides, parallel to the perforation. « Formed as a table » would not do in Dutch.

Lenticular (n° 5) — in the shape of a lens — is very often used for a short, biconvex bicone.

The blue cornerless cube (n° 11) is one of the oldest shapes of beads that were pressed in a form or « moulded ».

The cornerless hexagonal (variant of n°^{s} 10 and 12), dark blue with a white circle around the perforation, was distributed by Captain Cook on his voyage round the world and is known in large parts of Africa as the «ambassador bead », as it was very costly in the old days and served as a kind of passport for bearers of messages between tribal chiefs.

Collared beads (n° 14) are very rare outside India and Pakistan.

Faceted beads of glass (n°^{s} 17-18) are always moulded (pressed in a form). Those of stone are much more irregular, being ground on a stone.

Spacing beads (n°^{s} 22-24) are used when many strings are worn, to keep the different lines of beads neatly apart.

The pentagon bead (n° 25) is very dear to me as it often is of a beautiful amber colour and is one of the types from the 17th-century Amsterdam factory (p. 110) which spread farthest afield.

D. ORNAMENTED BEADS

Up to now we have studied only the shape of the beads, but all these forms may be adorned or ornamented with different colours and many patterns. These ornaments are only rarely painted on the surface of the bead. Nearly always they are applied lines or dots or stripes of different coloured glass, sometimes left in relief, at other times marvered flush with the surface.

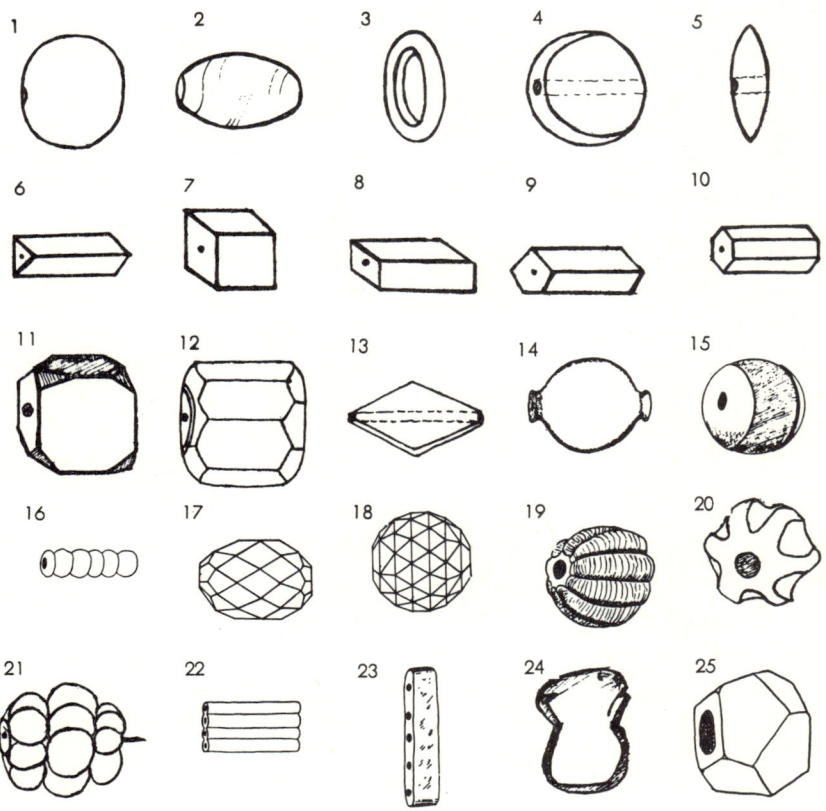

Fig. 5

Some special shapes of beads.

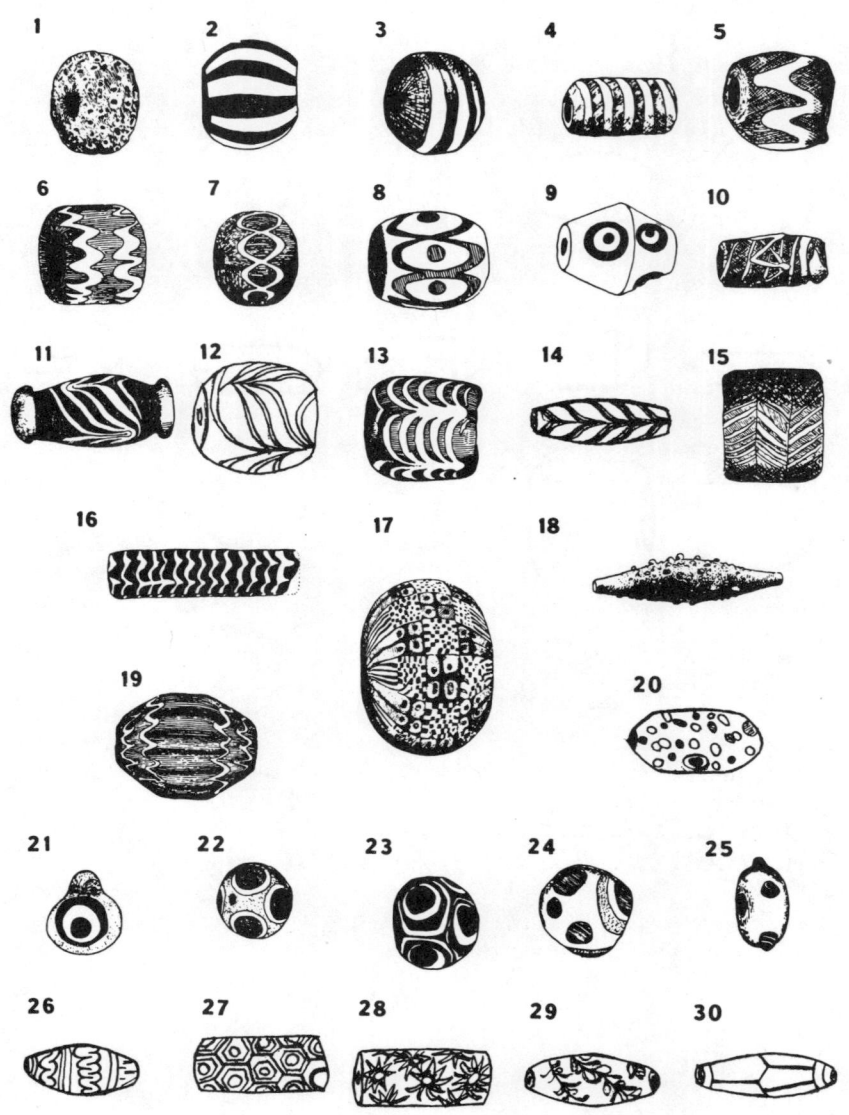

Fig. 6

Some types of ornamented beads.

In this way drawn beads can be ornamented with longitudinal stripes parallel to the perforation by a very simple procedure. When the hollow bulb of glass is formed it is rolled on a marver, on which half molten rods of coloured glass have been laid. When marvering, these rods are picked up by the hollow glass bulb, heated and reheated and marvered again, till the rods and the bulb have become a uniform mass. Then the drawing out begins and every rod gives a coloured stripe along the whole length of the drawn tube. This is cut or chopped into small lengths, that can be smoothed at the edges to become beads. The great mass of striped Italian and Czechoslovakian beads is made in this way.

All the other ornamented beads are made one by one by hand, by applying strips and dots of all colours to the surface of wound beads.

The wound bead (fig. 1) is made by turning a half molten rod of, for instance, light blue glass around an iron or copper wire. When the ring is complete around the wire, the rest of the rod is cut off and the bead is turned and heated till the junction is no longer visible and the round bead is well finished off. Then the woman takes a very thin, half molten rod of white glass and applies two white undulating strips around the top and base of the bead. Round the middle of the bead she lays a meandering line of gold-coloured glass. Next, five small red dots and a white spot in the middle form a rose. Four such roses are made at equal distances, a few green leaf spots are added and the bead is laid aside to cool. Instantly a new blue bead is started and exactly three minutes later a second ornamented rose-garlanded bead joins the first. I have watched this process myself in a small house on one of the Venetian canals, but the woman was known to be an expert worker. It is very difficult to find apprentices for this kind of work and that is the reason why many types of beads are disappearing from the catalogues. Soon machines will be constructed which can do some of the simplest jobs, but with the disappearance of manual work part of the beauty of these intricate forms of glass jewelry will disappear too. I am glad that I have seen this beautiful handwork in full swing.

In the accompanying glossary of types of ornamented beads I call nº 1 a spotted bead, but it could just as well be called a multiple eye-bead. It is only one of the many types of spotted beads. Some are decorated with just two or three, or perhaps more round spots of different colour from that of the body of the bead. Others may be black with about a dozen white spots, each with a red and bluish spot in the centre. These beads are used nowadays to pay for local products like palm-oil and rattan.

Glossary of types of ornamented beads (fig. 6, p. 42)

English	Français	Deutsch
1 spotted bead	perle mouchetée	gesprenkelte Perle
2 striped bead	perle striée	längsgestreifte Perle
3 zoned bead	perle zonée	quergestreifte Perle
4 bead with spiral lines	perle à spirale	Perle mit Spirale
5 bead with undulating line	perle à bande ondée	Perle mit Wellenlinie
6 bead with 2 undulating lines	perle à double bande ondée	Perle mit doppelter Wellenlinie
7 bead with 2 crossed undulating lines	perle à double bandes ondées entre lacées	Perle mit Achterschleifen
8 bead with 2 undulating lines and spots	perle à 2 ondes entrelacées et points centraux	Perle mit Achterschleifen und Punkten
9 bead with dot in circle	avec point dans cercle	mit Punkt in Kreis
10 scrabble bead	perle à lignes entremêlées	Perle mit allerhand Linien
11 ogee bead	perle à filets festonnés	Perle mit Kragen und Linien
12 ogee bead	perle à filets festonnés	Perle mit gothischen Bogenlinien
13 scallop bead	perle à arêtes de poissons	Perle mit Bogenreihen
14 palm-leaf, fern or feather bead	perle à décor de plumes	Perle mit Palmblattmuster
15 zigzag bead	perle à zigzags	Zick-zackperle
16 combed bead	perle à décor peigné	Perle mit Gekämmtenringen
17 chequer bead	perle chamarrée	Schachbrettperle

Italiano	Nederlands	Polski
1 punteggiata	gespikkeld	paciorek nakrapiany
2 rigata	gestreept	paciorek z podłużnymi pasmami
3 a fascie	geringd	paciorek z poprzecznymi pasmami
4 a spirale	met spiraallijnen	paciorek z linią spiralną
5 ondulata	met golflijn	paciorek z linią falistą
6 a due onde	met twee golflijnen	paciorek z podwójną linią falistą
7 a due onde incrociate	met twee gekruiste golflijnen	paciorek z przecinającymi się dwoma liniami falistymi
8 a due onde incrociate e punti	met 2 golflijnen en stippen	paciorek z przecinającymi się dwoma liniami falistymi i punktami
9 a circolo e punto	met cirkel en stip	z punktem w kole
10 con scarabocchi	met krabbels	paciorek z różnokierunkowymi liniami
11 con motivo ogivale	ojief kraal op en neergekamd	paciorek z lekko esowatymi liniami
12 con motivo ogivale	ojief kraal wijd gekamd	paciorek z lekko esowatymi liniami
13 con festoni	kraal met uitschulpingen	paciored z łukowatymi liniami
14 a piuma	4 × gekamd palmbladkraal op en neergekamd	paciorek z wzorem paprociowym
15 con zigzag	zigzagkraal	paciorek z linią zygzakowatą
16 con motivo a pettine	gekamde kraal	paciorek z linią lekko falistą
17 a scacchi	schaakbordkraal	paciorek z wzorem szachownicowym

English	Français	Deutsch
18 crumb bead (raised)	perle à granules saillants	Perle mit gekörnter Oberflächte
19 star or chevron bead	perle à chevrons	Chevronperle
20 crumb bead (smooth)	perle à granules lisses	Perle mit eingelegten Stücken
21 eye pendant	pendentif ocellé	Augenperle mit öse
22 stratified eye-bead	perle ocellée stratifiée	Perle mit unterlegtem Auge
23 stratified eye-bead	perle ocellée stratifiée	Perle mit doppelt unterlegtem Auge
24 stratified eye-bead with spots	perle avec yeux et points	Augenperle mit Punkten
25 horned eye-bead	perle ocellée à mammelons	perle mit aufgesetzten Augen
26 « Syrian » bead	perle « syrienne »	«syrische » Perle
27 mosaic bead	perle mosaïquée	Mosaikperle
28 millefiori bead	perle millefiori	millefiori Perle
29 arabesque bead	perle à arabesques	Arabeskeperle
30 etched bead	perle gravée à l'acide	geätste Perle

N⁰ 2, the striped bead, is the only ornamented bead that can as well be wound as drawn. Practically all the others in this list are wound beads, inlaid by hand on one bead after the other, except the chevron or star beads (n⁰ 19).

N⁰ 3, the zoned bead, has rings of other glass marvered into its surface.

The so-called combed beads, such as n⁰ˢ 11, 12, 13, 14, 16, are interesting forms. All these have first been surrounded by circles of thin glass rods. When they were still only adhering to the surface, the rings were pulled down with a little stick or comb and then fixed by marvering them into the surface. The ogee and the scallop beads as well as the

Italiano	Nederlands	Polsky
18 con granuli in rilievo	kruimelkraal met uitstekels	paciorek z reliefowym ornamentem ziarnistym
19 rosetta	chevronkraal	paciorek z ornamentem « wilczych kłów »
20 perla liscia a granuli	kruimelkraal glad	paciorek z wtapianymi plamkami
21 pendaglio con motivo occhio	ooghanger	paciorek oczkowaty z uszkiem
22 perla con occhio stratificata	gelaagde oogkraal	paciorek z warstwowanymi oczkami
23 perla con occhio doppi stratificata	dubbel gelaagde oogkraal	paciorek z podwójnie warstwowanymi oczkami
24 perla a occhi stratificata e punti	oogkraal met punten	paciorek z warstwowanymi oczkami i punktami
25 perla con occhi sporgenti	gehoornde oogkraal	paciorek z guzkami
26 perla « siriana »	« syrische » kraal	paciorek « syryjski »
27 perla mosaica	mozaiekkraal	paciorek mozaikowy
28 perla millefiori	millefiorikraal	paciorek millefiori
29 perla arabescata	arabeskkraal	paciorek z ornamentem arabeski
30 perla incisa all' acqua forte	geëtste kraal	paciorek szliforwany

palm-leaf or fern or feather type (n°s 12-14), are often found in modern Venetian wares. They may be combed up and down, or several times down, in a great variety of ways.

N° 17, the chequer bead. In the first millennium of our era it was the custom to melt a certain number of thin rods together, surrounding them with another kind of glass and then pulling them out into drawn rods about 3 mm. in diameter. Small slices cut from these rods would show very intricate figures and could be melted together in a glass matrix, nicely placed one next to the other. In that way astonishing results could be reached like the chequer-bead (n° 17) and the mosaic and millefiori beads, n°s 27 and 28.

Nº 19, the chevron, rosette or star bead. These beads are famous, because they have been found many times in west Africa in the possession of the chiefs and have also often been found by digging or working the fields. Another two were found in an Egyptian temple. So they were said to be ancient Egyptian. I first saw these beads as an ornament on one of the many gates in the large, world-famous glass factory, the Società Veneziana Conterie e Cristallerie. The president of the society, Gr. Uff. Dott. Michelangelo Pasquato, told me that these very large beads were used, for example, for ornamenting the reins of Bedouin camels and donkeys, and we know that the priests and monks who came to Egypt with Napoleon used the Theban temples as stables for their mounts. So much for their being ancient Egyptian.

It is very remarkable that up to now the star beads have not been found in datable surroundings, except when I found them amongst many other beads in the debris of a 17th-century glass and bead factory in the heart of Amsterdam. Venice still made them a few years ago, but has since stopped doing so because there, too, the wages are getting too high for everything that takes too much manual labour. Most of the ornamented beads will soon disappear. I repeat that I am glad I have seen the factory as well as the house-work in full swing.

Nos 21-25 are called eye-beads. Nº 21 is more a pendant than a bead. It was and is used as an ornament on donkey reins and saddles and tails as a beneficent eye, to chase away the influence of the evil eye. The type is old, as it has been found at Tell el Amarna, in black and white glass, dating about 1365 B.C., while it is still made in blue and yellow in Venice and in Hebron. All the other eye-beads are also, in the first place, amulets and often objects of great beauty. The eyes may be just simple round spots of colour, but very often they consist of different layers of glass. A black or dark spot on a white ground already gives much more the impression of a real eye and then we call the result a stratified eye-bead. The eyes may be slices of rods that have been pushed and marvered deep into the matrix, so that the whole bead feels smooth all over; in another type they may be felt as small protuberances, giving the bead a squarish form, or they may stick out, so that we can speak of horned beads. Variety enough; but most of these beads are found in the near east, the Mediterranean and central and western Europe and may be dated from 600 or 500 B.C. down to A.D. 400.

Nº 26 is what I call a Syrian bead. You may meet the type in Syria, Jordan, Persia and Israel; a few come from Aquileia. They are generally made of a black glass with white or yellow strips in the form of undulating lines or zigzags. The glass deteriorates easily. They can be placed in the first centuries of our era.

N°s 27 and 28 are types of mosaic and millefiori beads that have been fabricated in huge quantities in Venice specially for west Africa in the last four or five centuries. In the first centuries of our era you will often meet with red-capped beads, that show round the middle a green band with yellowish flowers or leaves.

N° 29 I call the arabesque bead as it is adorned with sprays, bearing leaves and/or flowers, which remind me of Pompeii as well as of the Taj Mahal and what is called the *cinquecento* in Italy. It is a real Venetian type spread all over the world in the last two or three centuries by explorers such as Stanley, who took this type of bead with him on his search for Livingstone.

N° 30 is not glass but cornelian, which was etched by soda or by a manganese compound, making white or black lines on the reddish bead. These beads, however, have often been imitated in glass, generally white inlaid on black, in the near east. The cornelian etched beads most probably come from India, where they were used from the 3rd millennium B.C. or earlier down to A.D. 200. I know them only from India and Persia and Sumerian Mesopotamia, while the common cornelian beads are found all over Asia and Africa; they are rare in Europe.

Some people may be looking in this list for the term « aggry beads ». In the old days Dapper ([1]) wrote about a precious bead, a light blue cylinder, that must have come from the sea and was supposed to be a kind of coloured coral. Later investigations by Mauny ([2]), Director of the Museum in Dakar, showed that all kinds of coloured beads, specially those worn by kings and priests, were called aggry beads. They also often come from tombs and amongst them sometimes were chevron beads, often called star beads in England. Kisa ([3]) gave as illustration of the aggry bead a picture of a star- or chevron-bead and most German writers have since copied his mistake. Nobody knows what the aggry beads of the 17th century really were.

([1]) DAPPER, O. (1676), *Nauwkeurighe beschrijvinghe der Afrikaanse gewesten* (Amsterdam).
([2]) MAUNY, R. (1949), « Perles de cornaline, quartz et verre des tumuli du Bas Sénégal », *Notes Africaines*, XLIII, 72-74.
([3]) KISA, A. (1908), *Das Glas im Altertume* (Leipzig), 134 ff., fig. 32.

E. COLOURED BEADS

One of the most important and at the same time almost impossible tasks is to describe the colour of a bead. There is such an enormous difference between a brilliantly shining, transparent bead and an opaque lustreless bead with the same chemical composition, that it is practically impossible to recognize them as being coloured by the same amount of the same agent. There are several colour guides to be found in bookshops and libraries, some of them giving several thousands of different colours, but it is much better to keep to a few dozen, for instance, those given in *Stanley Gibbons Colour Guide for Stamp Collectors*, to be bought at Stanley Gibbons Ltd., 391 Strand, London, W.C.2. I fear, however, that it may not be of much help. You need a painter's eye for this kind of work and they have a vocabulary entirely of their own.

CHAPTER V

Classification of beads

« Classification is the arrangement of things in classes according to the characteristics they have in common ». So says the *Encyclopaedia Britannica* (1964), vol. V, p. 883 *a*.

H.C. Beck [1] based his classification entirely on the forms of his beads and pendants, but I cannot agree with that in sorting out my own collection. Putting all my spherical beads together in a row, and then the oval and after that, for instance, the square ones could never lead to any conclusion. All large collections in the first place answer two questions « from where » and « when », so that we can know the distribution of a certain group of beads geographically and in time. Secondly we may ask if the beads are made where they are found, or if they have travelled far and wide, showing us the trade-routes of times past.

In the second part of this handbook, therefore, my classification will in the first place be geographical, putting together the beads from one country, and as far as possible beginning with the oldest beads available.

Of course I can only record what I have been able to find out myself and what I could gather in the museums which I have visited in the last 15 or 20 years and in the literature. I hope that my comments may bring me numerous particulars from many readers, so that soon hereafter a much more complete review may be published.

---

[1] BECK, H.C. (1928).

PART TWO

What is known about beads and their distribution

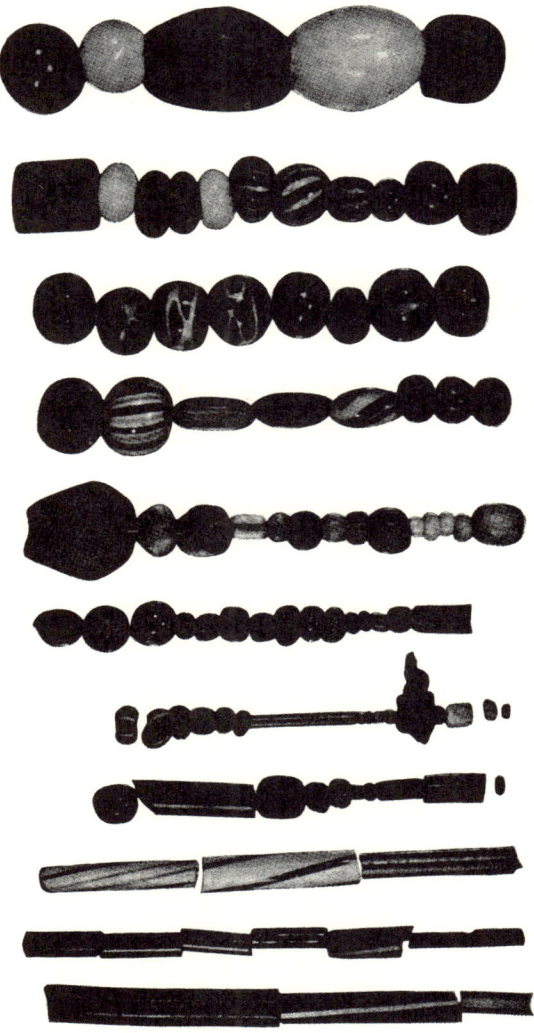

GLASS BEADS AND THE TUBES from which they are made, all actual size, collected from fields in 's Graveland, near Naarden-Bussum, south-east of Amsterdam. First row on top shows large wound beads in blue and white, probably the oldest of the series. Second row has five wound beads — the first a pentagonal cylinder, an old form — then six drawn beads with coloured stripes, which may show Venetian influence. In third row are wound, handmade, beads with wavy lines and stripes. Fourth row has drawn beads of different types; fifth row, handmade wound beads, including pentagons. Remaining six rows are composed of drawn beads and tubes, mostly striped.

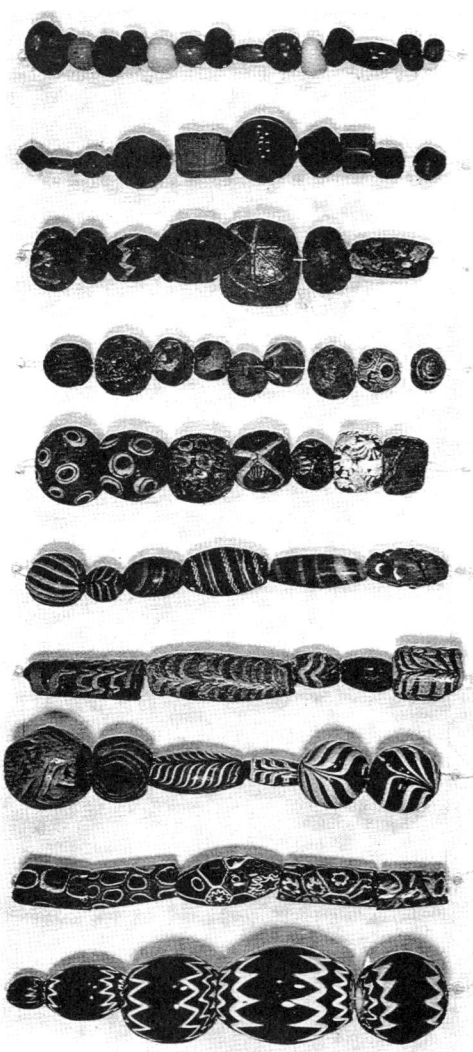

First row. Early ancient beads are all unicoloured and spherical or oval in shape. They may be yellow, green, blue, red or black. — *Second row.* The shape can later be changed to flat beads, collared beads, facetted ones, square cylinder beads, melon beads, pentagon beads, hexagonal cylinder beads, pentagonal bicones, etc., etc. — *Third row.* Beads can be ornamented with white or yellow lines of different forms, or by melting in crumbs of green, red, white or blue glass (Crumb beads, from 4th cent. B.C. to 9th cent. A.D.). — *Fourth row.* Eye-beads with a few « eyes » from 4th cent. B.C. and later. — *Fifth row.* Beads with many eyes, sometimes protruding, then A.D. Many occur in Merovingian times. — *Sixth row.* Ornamented beads with stripes, zones and spirally wound lines and arabesque beads. — *Seventh row.* Combed beads from the beginning of our era until Merovingian times. — *Eighth row.* Modern combed beads, mostly from Venice. — *Ninth row.* Mosaic and millefiori beads from modern times, but already known in Roman times. — *Tenth row.* Modern Chevron, Star or Rosetta beads, common from Venice and from 17th-century Amsterdam. The type is certainly not Egyptian.

CHAPTER I

Prehistoric Beads

Teeth, bits of bones, shells, seeds, pieces of stalactite tubes or porcupine quills and in fact all pierceable objects up to the hardest semi-precious and even precious stones, were worn around neck and ankles, arms and toes as ornaments or, what is perhaps more important, as amulets.

It appears that the very oldest objects that were pierced and strung were small marine molluscs, such as were found on the skull of Grimaldi-Man, about 100,000 years old. Not much younger will be the front tooth of a horse, which I found in a Solutréan cave, pierced through the root and adorned with three horizontal stripes on the enamel (fig. 1). Next, in my collection, is a set of wolf's teeth, alternating with bits of stalactite of late palaeolithic age, perhaps 10,000 years old, to judge from the stone tools found with it in a cave near Ceyrac in the Cevennes (France). Nowadays Papuans, deep in the jungle, often wear necklaces of teeth, not only of their prey — boar's and dog's tusks and teeth — but also of their foes, often as human as they are themselves. As a rule we do not consider all these as being beads, unless they are worked into regular forms out of stones and minerals, as well as jet, amber, cornelian, bits of eggshell or even pottery.

In western Europe very favourite ornaments were beads of amber, but these disintegrate rather quickly in moist soil. They may be found from c. 2000 B.C. to medieval times. They soon disappear when cornelian and glass are imported from the near east. Dr. Arkell (1936) proved that the factory in Cambay (India) worked from 3000 B.C. up to the present time, making the same types of beads for 5000 years.

But do not think that teeth as ornaments have disappeared from the jewel-cases of our day. Just as the American Indian likes to hang on his breast the tusk of the great grizzly bear he has mastered, so the European hunter who has killed a beautiful stag will have the eyetooth cut out and mounted in gold and will offer it to the lady of his choice as a pendant for her evening dress.

After shells and teeth, cornelian, as already mentioned, is certainly the most important material. Families in Holland are named « *Korallen-slijper*» after their handiwork of a few hundred years ago. In England

55

their name would have been « Beadcutter ». It must be explained that the Dutch word « *kraal* » is derived from coral, meaning the red coral that was much used in Holland for necklaces a thousand years ago, but it now means a glass bead. We talk about « *gitkralen* » for jet-beads and use the word in « *cornalijnen kralen* » as well. Red coral is called « *bloedkoraal* ».

Cornelian beads have never been studied thoroughly. They have spread all over the world in the last 7000 years, often in raw pieces that had to be ground in the port of entry. In fact in the cargo-lists of ships of our East Indian Company, available in the State Archives in The Hague there is frequent mention of boxes of stones. On the coast of east and south Africa one often finds small pebbles of agate and cornelian of thumb-nail size, but not yet pierced, parts of the load of many European ships, that were lost in those waters, but specially on the coast of Natal, in the 17th and 18th centuries. Nearly all great-grandmothers of our times possessed necklaces of beautiful, rounded cornelians, mostly ground to multifaceted beads, in all colours from milk-white to red. I should like some student of mineralogy to investigate these cornelian beads. Cornelian beads were fabricated in Idar Oberstein (Germany) in Roman times, though the great mass always came from Cambay in Gujerat. Nowadays the German workshops all use material imported from Brazil. Many people from Idar-Oberstein emigrated to that country when their old mines at home were exhausted. In their new abode they found agates in such quantities that nearly all of them returned to Europe to pick up their old trade with the treasures sent from the New World. Fashion, too, plays a role just as much in stone beads as in lace or silk. The form of cornelian beads changes with time and place. Globular ones will be found everywhere in many different sizes. Oval beads often come from Egypt, cylinder beads, twelve mm. long, are very common on the Great Island (Madagascar). Tabular beads I know only from Persia, short truncated hexagonal bicones are typical of the middle ages in Jordan and Syria. Long hexagonal bicones penetrate far into the Indian Ocean, and there are square bicones, standard and long, in my collection which come from 8th- to 10th-century sites in Indonesia and Malacca.

We must always write about cornelian and agate together, because they are products of the same process. When molten rock like lava solidifies into basalt, andesite or melaphyr, large holes are formed and in the course of millions of years these holes are filled up by quartz, chalcedony, calcite, etc., which are deposited from aqueous solutions, that always penetrate even the hardest rocks.

Layer after layer of these minerals are deposited, often in the form of very fine crystals. Some layers will be clear and transparent, others may be milky white, still others may be coloured yellow to red by iron, dissolved in the fluids penetrating the rocks. In this way the holes may become quite filled, the centre of the « agate » often being of one colour and formed from beautiful, large crystals. If the inside of the agate is reddish to red we call that part cornelian.

Of course Cambay did not export only cornelians and agates. It also produced beautifully-worked beads of quartz, onyx, amethyst, garnet, etc. It cannot be proved that glass beads were ever made there.

CHAPTER II

Beads from Mesopotamia

The history of beads probably begins in the near east several thousand years before Christ, where necklaces have been found in strata equal in age with the lowest and most ancient remains of dwelling places in the most ancient town on earth, Jericho. In those days, the neolithic culture was already widespread, as traces have been found on Cyprus as well as in Anatolia. In Nicosia Museum (Cyprus) a necklace, dated by carbon 14 as having been used about 5500 B.C., is made of Dentalium shells, alternating with beautifully-polished cornelian beads, which shows that jewelry was of a high standard seven and a half thousand years ago.

And yet the people who worked these hard stones into spherical polished beads and traded them from India to the Mediterranean did not even know how to make and fire a clay pot ! Pottery was still unknown 7000 years ago. Later, in the 5th millennium B.C., the Sumerians, who gave names to the stars, that are still used, and to the signs of the zodiac, continued to trade cornelians from Cambay in Gujerat and lapis lazuli from their northern neighbours. Around 4000 B.C. in Mesopotamia these semi-precious stones began to be imitated in faience and a few hundred years later in glass or in glazed quartz.

When Sir Leonard Woolley excavated the Royal Cemetery at Ur, he found that in the early part of the third millennium B.C. the fine arts had developed masterpieces in stone, bronze, gold and wood. Beads were much used, but they were nearly all made of gold or semi-precious stones like cornelian and lapis lazuli; later came faience and later still glass.

Now on p. 21 I said that Russian and Polish archaeologists record glass beads from the third millennium B.C. in the south Caucasus, a region well known for its early knowledge of metallurgy. The old coppersmiths may have seen the first glass in the slags of their copper-melting furnaces. They knew about furnaces and heating to high temperatures, knowledge necessary for the making of glass.

Of the old glass-works of Syria only Hebron still has a working glass-factory, but, just as in Damascus and in Aleppo, they produce only very crude work, vases, beakers, ash-trays, etc., and even beads, but mostly large, heavy, square blocks of wildly-wound glass. For a long time, too, they have been making a kind of eye-bead pendant in yellow and blue, very much like a Tell el Amarna type, used now specially to protect donkeys from the evil eye. But they make nothing like the beautiful eye-beads that played such a large rôle in the last five centuries B.C.

From Bezborodov and other writers in Slavonic languages (Bobrova, Chmielovska, Dekovna, Hensel, Krumphanzlova, Lwowa, etc. — see Bibliography, p. 121) we can learn a lot more about Mesopotamian and other near eastern beads, but mostly those of later times. In Garni, the old residence of the Armenian kings, in the 2nd and 3rd centuries A.D., not only beads, but glass window-panes and many glass vessels were made. This also happened in Azerbaijan in the last two centuries B.C. There is no doubt that, though Syrian glass was imported to both these places, they had their own glass-factories also. In Georgia, Armenia, Azerbaijan and Tashkent many glass-factories worked all through the first centuries of our era up to the 11th and 12th centuries A.D.

The same is true in Afrasiab, the old Samarkand, where Timurlane brought together all the artisans he took from Syria, Jordan, etc. From there as well as from the Caucasus many beads went north over the Black Sea and instigated the building of glass-works in Opole, Krakov, Wroclaw, and Kruzwicka in Poland. Their first products were, usually, mosaic-cubes, then window-panes for the churches and after that beads, just as history tells us happened in medieval Venice.

It is interesting that in the 7th century B.C. glass was made in Mesopotamia from one part sand and three parts ashes of Chenopodiae, salt-loving plants that grow very well in the desert, whereas the first real Russian glass, from the 8th to 12th century A.D., contained 25 to 75 % of lead, perhaps owing to a lack of alkaline salts.

Beads are said to be very plentiful in the near east, but I have not been lucky enough to meet them in any quantity. In the museums of Jerusalem, Amman or Damascus, you may find a few dozen on exhibition. Even in the large and beautiful museum in Cairo beads are rarely exhibited. Until quite recently nobody really studied beads. As they must have been used for trading and barter now for about ten thousand years, future students always have the chance of finding a host of new facts, that may be most important for our knowledge of trade and trade-routes.

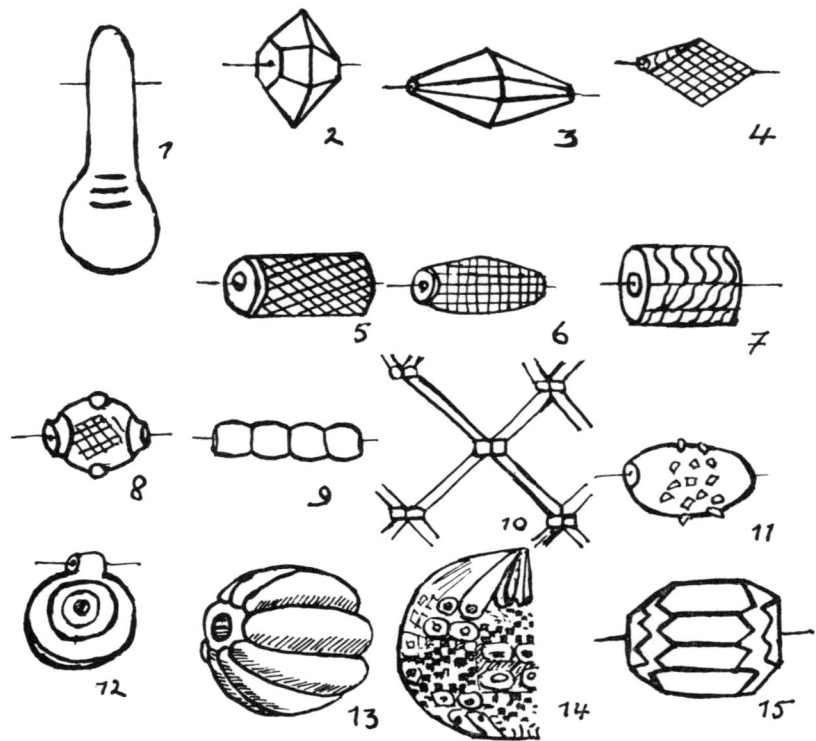

PLATE I, figs. 1-15
Types of prehistoric and ancient beads.

CHAPTER III

Egyptian Beads

Before Narmer and Menes, the founders of the 1st Dynasty, there are several predynastic cemeteries in which we encounter, perhaps as first signs of art or civilization, necklaces of beads. They are mostly very simple objects such as small round discs, cut out of ostrich-egg shells, just like those still made nowadays by the African Bushmen. Soon, however, soft stones were cut into cylinders and perforated to make, e.g., beads of amazonite, a soft felspar, called microalin by the mineralogists. Before Narmer (3000 B.C.), however, we meet with cornelian beads that must have been imported from India, and lapis lazuli cylinders that must have been brought from Mesopotamia. Trade and commerce probably spread all over the near east at this early time.

Even the very well known faience beads may first have been imported from Mesopotamia and soon imitated in upper Egypt. Pulverized quartz or fine sand was mixed with a little lime or alkali to a kind of paste and then heated after having been kneaded or moulded around a small stick or combustible stem, which, when burnt away, left a perforation. This faience forms most of the beads found throughout Pharaonic times. Perhaps the best known forms are the slender blue cylinder beads some 20 mm. long and 2 1/2 mm. wide, that are known as mummy-net beads, because they form a net over the mummy-coffins of the 18th to 23rd Dynasties, as, e.g., in Tutankhamun's tomb (1352 B.C.) (fig. 10). These small beads became of special interest to me when I observed that many of them were different at the two ends. At one end they were broken off, so that the white faience core was visible with a very thin blue glaze over it, while at the other end no white appeared, the end of the bead being just a glassy blue. Investigation showed that such a bead was in fact half glass, half faience. Heating made it turn into glass all over. I next heated a faience bead with a little bit of soda, and the whole bead soon turned into clear blue glass. I thus came to the conclusion that glass was discovered when faience was heated too fiercely or had a little surplus alkali in the mixture. When, however, the material used for faience is too coarse, so that you can loosen the grains of sand with your finger-nail, we talk of frit (fig. 7).

Of course it is impossible to give a full description of all Egyptian beads here. There are two good collections in western Europe that may be of use to the student. In the Department of Egyptology, University College, Gower Street, London, W.C. 1, the collection of Sir Flinders Petrie is on view. Even more interesting is the collection in the Ashmolean Museum in Oxford. Here I can only give a few particulars.

Most Egyptian beads, specially those in faience, occur in the same types from Narmer to the Ptolemies. There are always many small disc- and ring-beads. Segmented beads are common even in predynastic graves (fig. 9). Lapis lazuli cylinders abound sometimes next to white and green cylinders of faience. During the 4th to 6th dynasties long narrow cylinders, 30 - 40 mm. long by 4 mm. diameter, in brown and blackish colours come into fashion. Smaller faience cylinders shine in nice blue and green colours, while very small green ringlets 2-3 mm. wide, alternate with cornelian ones. During the 9th dynasty we get more and more variation in the faience beads. Intricately woven collars of cylinder and oblate beads call for spacing beads and these are made in stone, faience or cornelian. Long barrels of faience, with crumbs of quartz, etc., in relief, we learned (p. 46) to call crumb-beads (fig. 18). Faience comes in larger forms, cylinders of 12-14 mm. diameter, with granulated surfaces, or flattened lozenges or tabular discs. The 10th dynasty brings small glazed melon beads of 10 mm. diameter and green globular beads with a black spot, that may be described as the first eye-beads. The 12th dynasty brings many elliptical and globular amethyst beads as imports and in general somewhat clearer colours in the faience. From these times, about 1800 B.C., we know how these long cylinders of faience, about 12 by 3 mm., were made, because an unfinished set of beads was found. Holes 12-15 mm. deep were made in a block of clay by pushing in a pencil-shaped bit of wood and then removing it. A small match-like stick was placed in the middle of each hole and around it the mixture of sand with some lime or alkali was inserted. When the clay block was fired the match-like sticks were burnt away and left a perforation in the centre of the bead

The 18th dynasty began *c.* 1580 B.C. and with it the New Empire. It looks as if this New Empire, at the top of its might, shakes loose all bonds and allows the arts and crafts to develop along quite other lines, no more drawing on the cult of the dead, but turning to the living things of nature like flowers and birds and other animals, enjoying their beauty, which makes stylization superfluous. A great industrial resurgence breaks forth and this had a special influence on the glass-industry. The glass-factories now produce artistic and beautiful beads and pendants, necklaces and bangles and small medicine or perfume flasks rather than drinking-vessels and larger bottles of practical use, which come into common use only in Roman times. All these products have an accomplished form and lustre that makes us wonder how a technique can develop and come to maturity in such a comparatively short time ([1]). And all this occurred not only in glass but in faience too. There are new forms, new colours, new combinations. Look for instance at the famous earrings of Tutankhamun with short biconical ring-beads in bright red, orange, green and blue, in glass as well as in faience. Small melon-beads and simple eye-beads are found and eye-pendants both in black and white and in blue glass with yellow rings just as they are made today in Hebron.

During the 20th-23rd dynasties the mummy-net beads and small oblates were made in very great numbers. They are about the only Egyptian beads which you often see as necklaces, but I fear that most of them, specially the very clear blue ones, are imitated in great quantities nowadays, like so many scarabs.

We will often see the words Egypt (Roman period) or Romano-Egyptian used in dating beads. One of the best known of these beads is a large, bluish-green faience melon bead, sometimes nearly 25 mm. in diameter. It is often found together with a deep-blue glass bead of the same form and same size. It is known from all the corners of the Roman Empire and even farther afield, but as usual nobody knows where these beads were made. There is always talk about Alexandria as a centre of the glass- and bead-industry in Roman times, but nothing exact is known about that. There is talk too, about Aquileia on the Adriatic, but no sure traces of the making of glass beads have yet been found there ([2]). Another strange fact is that in displays of finds from Pompeii you will see only the melon-beads (fig. 13), which I have just mentioned, and a few necklaces of quartz (rock-crystal) beads. In the Archaeological Department in the Baths of Diocletian (Terme Museum) in Rome a professor told me : « Glass beads ? The Romans used gold and silver and jewels. Glass was for the Barbarians! » I remembered at once, that I was blue eyed and had been fair.

([1]) Though we known that glass beads were made a thousand years earlier around the Caucasian mountains and the art of bead- and glass-working must have come to Egypt from the orient, there is no evidence of the manufacture of glass vessels, anywhere, before the 16th century B.C.

([2]) There is good evidence for Roman glassmaking in general at Aquileia. Cf. Carina CALVI « The Roman Glass from Northern Italy », Museum Haaretz (Tel Aviv), Bulletin no. 8 (June 1966), 55 ff. (espec. p. 59).

This is all we can say, it seems, about Egypt, Roman period.

But what, then, are the beads in beautiful colours and forms that make lovers of beauty pull out their purses and pay a high price? This is difficult to say, but I found in a nice museum collection, described as « Roman-Egyptian » chequer beads (fig. 14), mostly to be dated 8th or 9th century A.D. and chevron beads that cannot have been made before the 14th century. Indeed, it was partly faulty identifications of this kind that led me to think that a handbook on beads might be of use, although I know that my knowledge is far from complete. But it seems the only way to bring together all the existing knowledge about beads. Many of these beads are found in Syria and at Aquileia, too, and you may even pick them up on the Rhine. Fremersdorf (1955), for example, first thought that the beads he found on the Rhine had been made in Cologne, but later his thoughts, too, went farther and farther south towards Syria and Egypt, countries that had been visited by some of the Roman soldiers who died on the Limes.

This brings us to Merovingian beads, which are often quite comparable with material from round the Mediterranean and could very well have developed from Syrian predecessors. One of the next things to do is to study Byzantine and eastern European beads, bringing to bear, e.g., what we have already learned from Russian and Caucasian finds.

The Etruscans too at a much earlier date (earlier 1st millennium B.C.) may have brought knowledge of glass from their former oriental homes. But there is no certainty, yet, about this ([1]).

([1]) There is an interesting collection of glass beads, that ought to be described soon, in Aquileia, where, *inter alia*, much black glass occurs, too. Interesting black beads occur there, flattened with 3 or 4 parallel perforations, and many striped and combed beads and eye-beads as well. Some of these beads are certainly not B.C., but A.D.

CHAPTER IV

Phoenician and Punic Beads

About 1200 B.C. people of Canaanite descent settled on the northwestern coast of Syria and northern Palestine. They soon developed into a seafaring people, trading along the coasts of the Mediterranean, bartering the products of the east for whatever they wanted from the west. They also exploited the vanity of men and women and offered them clothes (textiles), and beads made from semi-precious stones, faience and glass. They built warehouses in favourable spots, which sometimes grew into colonies such as those that have now become the towns of Tunisia and Ibiza. And just like the Amsterdam merchants in the 17th century A.D., the Phœnicians two or three thousand years earlier built factories to make glass beads and trinkets and possibly vessels as well, and used them to pay for the other wares they needed. Artisans came over to the colonies and worked there in the old ways, but adding new forms welcome to their new customers. No wonder that in these colonies we get a better chance of retrieving the old merchandise than we do in the motherland, that was so much more frequently subject to the changes of history. That is why we went to Carthage and Ibiza, to see the archaeological finds made there.

About 30 minutes ride by car from Tunisia, on the top of the Hill of St-Louis at Carthage lies a monastery housing the Lavigerie Museum. There can be seen what the White Fathers (the famous Pères Blancs) have collected in excavating Punic tombs at Carthage ranging from the 7th to the 2nd century B.C. What will strike you first are a dozen large glass pendant-beads, 50 mm. high, resembling masks of bearded people (fig. 16) with yellow lips and fierce blue eyes : another such pendant pictures a ram's head, the ram being the favourite offering to Baal Hammon, as the all-destroying god of the Carthaginians was called.

A second group of beads (?) of about the same size are large cylinders about 18 mm. diameter, with a wall no more than 3 mm thick. A thick row of protruding eyes runs all round the equator of the beads and several rows of smaller eyes, all protruding, all in yellow on a light blue ground, finish this elaborate bit of work (fig. 17 and 20).

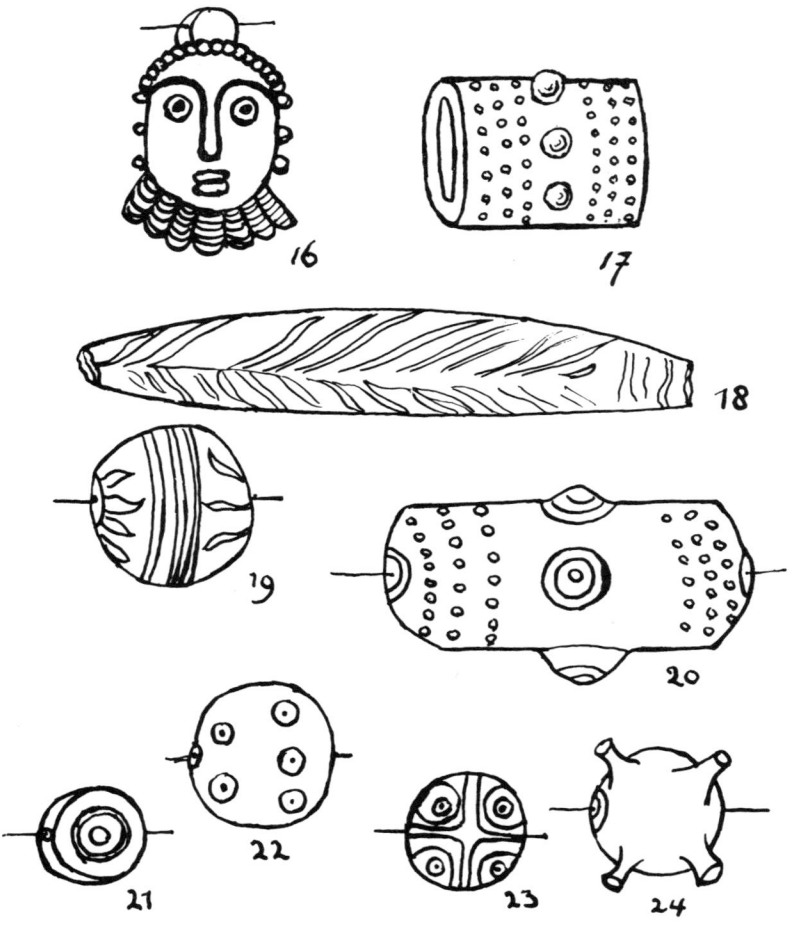

PLATE II, figs. 16-24.
Glass beads and pendant from Carthago and Persia.

Then follow eye-beads and more eye-beads, some very simple, some very intricate, but not yet the so-called stratified beads, the pupils of the eyes being surrounded by only a white or yellow ring and nothing more.

My impression was that the human-head beads were mostly made in Carthage, but, when an exhibition of ancient jewelry was held in Venice, there were many of them, not only from Tunisia or even Syria, but equally from north-eastern Italy, Anatolia, Palestine and Egypt. It had struck me already on Ibiza that there were many typical Egyptian amulets there. Ibiza was a Carthaginian colony and in the museum you will find a remarkable mixture of Egyptian, Carthaginian, Syrian and Mesopotamian glass and faience.

There is a third group of glass and faience beads of Punic type also, namely long ovate to cylindrical beads, striped or zoned or combed, ornamented with white or yellow lines or simply twirled to give an interesting or even beautiful appearance. From my drawings it can be seen that some of these beads were 10 cm. long (fig. 18).

In the Bardo Museum in Tunisia and in the Archaeological Museum in Barcelona there is much Punic material, awaiting study and publication.

We must now move in our next chapter to the heart of the middle east — to Persia, or Iran, as it is now called. Carthage was colonized from Syria by a princess of Tyre, a town that has played an important rôle in the history of glass. But nowhere in the Syro-Palestinian area — neither in Jerusalem, nor in Jericho or Amman, nor in Damascus — have I been able to find a large collection of glass or faience beads. If it is true, as people say, that a huge amount of beads is to be found everywhere in the near east, their collection and study has clearly been neglected. The same is true in Egypt. In Cairo the famous museum contains (it seems) no real collection of beads, and in Alexandria with its traditional fame as a glass-centre practically no beads or other glass objects are to be found. In Persia however there are many Phœnician beads and we must study them.

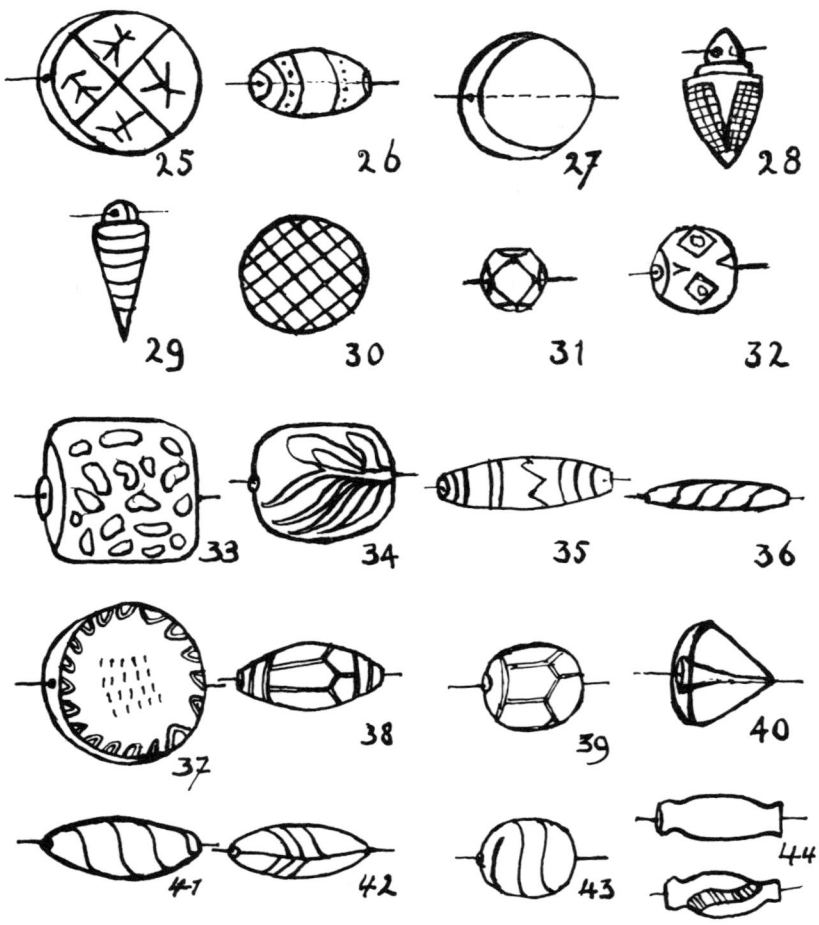

PLATE III, figs. 25-44
Beads from Persia and India.

CHAPTER V

Beads from Persia

During the last two years many necklaces and other strings of beads from Persia have found their way to Europe, for it is rather easy, around Teheran and other towns, to lay hands on strings of beads and pendants that catch the eye of the archaeologist.

There are, among these beads, an extraordinarily large number of cornelians. These are not just the large and small globular beads that abound in so many countries; there is a preponderance of rather rare forms.

There are, firstly, etched beads (fig. 25-26), which show lines and dots and some more intricate figures in white or black, depending on whether natron or some manganese compound has been used to etch the surface, the rest of the bead being covered by wax, a method we know so well from batik work in Indonesia. This way of adorning beads was practised in India as early as about 4000 years ago.

Nearly all cornelian beads were made in Cambay, Gujerat Province. This factory has been working for 7000 years (p. 18) and its products exist not only all over Europe and Asia, but also on the old caravan routes through the Sahara, which even today serve Lake Chad and Kano. There the natives will bring globular and oval beads and square biconical pyramids, while the long hexagonal bipyramids go to the east coast of Africa and all down the coasts around the Indian Ocean.

In Persia, however, we find many tabular beads, circular (fig. 27), but with two flat sides parallel to the perforation. There are also drop-pendants (fig. 29), or pendants looking like a bunch of grapes (fig. 28), melon-beads of cornelian, but no pentagonal or hexagonal cylinders, such as are often found in far eastern countries. A very conspicuous variety is much younger, namely the multifaceted cornelian bead (fig. 30) found in all colours, from milky-white to black, and in all shades from light yellow to deep orange red. These probably date from 200-300 years ago at most and they can still be found in nearly all old Dutch families as heirlooms, dating from the times of the East India Company.

As Cambay, where all this cornelian comes from, is not so very far from Persia, we will not be astonished to find here many other products from its factories, such as beautifully-ground garnets, beads of lapis lazuli, jasper, quartz, onyx, agate and turquoise. We also find beautiful beads of granite, diorite, porphyry, felspar (amazonite or mikroalin), amongst which we might include the green-glazed quartz (fig. 31-32) that is more common in Persia than in Egypt.

Very numerous are beads, most of them probably locally made, of limestone and seashell, materials that are often difficult to distinguish without the use of a microscope and some stone-cutting device.

Much more important, however, for our studies are faience beads, which are very numerous and of very different form and design. I can mention only some typical forms and give a few pictures.

Some very interesting faience beads were brought to me with the information that they came from Amlash, an old town site just south of the Caspian Sea, and were said to be dated 2500 B.C. They are of coarse, white faience, that might perhaps better be called frit, and are ornamented with rings of black glass, that have been « combed » so that they are best described as ogee-pattern beads. Some look as if the material had first been burnt black and afterwards zoned white or inlaid with a white wavy line.

The more common forms of faience beads are found in Persia just as they are all over the orient — globular and cylinder beads, segmented beads and ringlets. Melon-beads occur too, but they are much smaller than those that occur all over southern Europe. They are probably imported from Egypt and are coloured dark brown. Some are flattened to short buttons. Flattened tubular beads, too, are numerous in some parts. More interesting are larger beads, up to 25 mm. long, with reticulated patterns, which are said to have originated in Mesopotamia and from there found their way to Egypt.

Another remarkable type has the form of a lozenge; yet another resembles the collared beads from India. One of these is squared and bears a dot-and-ring design, while others are pressed in a trigonal form and have pits on three sides, alternating with reticulate ribs.

We have seen that the composition of faience and glass beads varies only in the relative quantities of alkali and quartz in the mixture. Many intermediate forms are, thus, possible, specially as the furnaces in the old days could not be made as hot as we can make them now. Only in the 1st and the 2nd century B.C. have faience beads often been heated to such a degree, that the result could be called homogeneous, but they never become quite clear and diaphanous, so as to be called glass, which we define as a mixture of sand and lime with soda or potash, which melts into a homogeneous mass.

Glass beads are very numerous in Persian graves and tombs, but as so many have been found in non-scientific excavations, they are often difficult to date. The oldest may well be the cobalt-blue oblates, 6 mm. in diameter, that are found nearly all over the world, but the beautifully scintillating, spirally-wound long oval beads, that abound in the middle east, might be equally old.

There are also a great many interesting « eye-beads ».

These eye-beads can vary greatly (see part I, fig. 6, n°s 21-25). They may have just one black spot on a white bead (fig. 21), or two, or three, or more of them. They may have one or two rows of eyes on the bead (fig. 22). They may even be stratified eye-beads (fig. 23), when the pupil is surrounded by a broad, white field with two or more brown lines, contrasting with the white. The eyes may be melted into the matrix without any protrusion, or they may sit on knobs (fig. 24) that make the bead triangular or square, for which reason we call them horned beads. The last invention on eye-beads, I think, was melting into the surface little discs or sticks, cut from a complicated rod, that showed, in section, something like an eye, often surrounded by radiating lines.

All these varieties of eye-beads have been studied in detail by G. Eisen (1916). He illustrates many and tries to arrange them in date order, but this seems to be asking too much of the evidence, though some of his, it is true, were carefully excavated and can be dated by potsherds and sometimes even by coins associated with them.

Happily, there are other places where similar beads have been found under very interesting conditions which give them a sure date in the 4th and 3rd centuries B.C.

One of the first ornaments, mostly on black beads, was a single wavy line, but soon there occur two wavy lines, first parallel, later crossing. Then the wavy lines were combined with light spots, that soon develop into eyes, or stayed, alternating with the spots, between the crossing points of the wavy lines. When this occurs, however, we are already far into Roman times, perhaps in the 2nd or 3rd century A.D. At the same time the eyes are no longer fused with the matrix of the bead, but often protrude, specially when the eyes are no longer built up of several layers to depict the whites and pupils, but are pieces of rod cut off, so that the section shows the pupil of the eye with its surround. In that case, the eyes stand on top of bosses.

The faience or glass melon-beads (fig. 13) so common elsewhere are very scarce in Persia and so are the Indian collared beads, and this gives the impression that there was far more export than import of beads in Persia. Among imports are probably the glass beads containing gold-leaf between two layers of clear glass. A very interesting export bead (fig. 33) is large (up to 25 mm. in length and diameter) with a greenish matrix and shows on the surface irregular circles and ovals and red loops with yellow inside or yellow loops with black inside. These occur in stone-age graves in Java, and turn up also in Sarawak, Malacca and Lop Nor (China). There are examples in several museums of Chinese art, although I believe they were not made in China, but were perhaps imitated there. They can be distinguished by a large content of lead and even barium. We find small specimens of the same technique in Persia too. For these beads see v. Heekeren (1958), Seligman and Beck (1938), Beck (1930), etc.

After Islam came to Persia another kind of bead develops, commonly called the Mameluke bead (fig. 34). This is a green bead with a yellow surface and on that surface many red or blue or orange-shaped lines in chevron or zigzag patterns.

CHAPTER VI

Beads from India

I came to India after a long search all over Europe for certain types of beads, which I had collected around Rhodesian ruins and on the island of Zanzibar, in an attempt to find out the origin of a large series of beads, nearly all opaque with very attractive pastel colours. I had never seen these beads being worn by girls in that part of Africa or sold in shops or markets. I had not found them in our museums, but when going through Indian literature, I found reason enough to seek them in the large museums at Calcutta and Allahabad and in private collections : and there they were in hundreds and thousands. Some had been very well described already by Beck (1941), others by Dikshit (1952).

As might be expected in India, there were very many stone beads and a good number of glass ones, as well as some of bone or shell or even pottery, but practically none of faience, a material that is so common in Mesopotamia, Egypt and Persia. The forms and colours of the glass beads, too, pointed to a development, independent from that in other neighbouring countries.

STONE BEADS

There are very few beads of precious stones, of course, but very many of semi-precious stones. As usual the cornelian beads are greatly in the majority, usually mixed with agates and onyxes. In India some of the cornelian beads are always etched with white or black lines or dots. This was done as early as 4000 years B.C. and was still practised in the first centuries of our era. Beads to be ornamented in this way are first covered with wax. The wax is removed where a line is desired and when the whole design is incised in the wax, the bead is treated with strong alkali to produce white lines (fig. 37) or with permanganate to produce black lines (fig. 38 and 39). Often the whole bead is whitened and then black lines are added or the whole bead blackened, to add white lines afterwards. We have met these etched beads already in Persia, but there, as far as I know, only white etched lines are known.

Crystal clear quartz beads in many forms and just as clear green-coloured beryl, the latter in Roman times worth its weight in gold, provide bright patches in many collections, while lapis lazuli and red as well as green jasper take care of the undertones. The jasper beads often have the form of half a circle. Some beautifully-worked garnet hexagonal and rectangular cylinders complete the list of stone beads in my collection, but other collections often contain emeralds and rubies.

GLASS BEADS

Indian glass beads include some very interesting special forms which are very rare elsewhere. The following are, I believe, the oldest varieties.

(a) *Hand-perforated beads*. These are made from globular balls of molten glass dropped on an earthenware disc or plate and then perforated with an iron nail. Where the nail penetrates the ball there is a wide funnel-shaped opening, while on the other side the opening is small and round. Often these globular beads are flattened (fig. 40). These beads are generally made of light green glass.

(b) *Multiple-wound beads*. These are made by winding a thin glass rod, half molten, several times around a conical core till a bead of 6-12 mm. diameter is attained (fig. 41).

(c) *Folded blue beads*, with white lines around the centre (fig. 42). These beads have the form of a squared cylinder, the line where the fold closes often being plainly visible, specially where the white lines do not exactly fit.

(d) *Black oblate beads with white or red spiral lines*.

(e) *Collared beads*. These beads, which have a ring-like collar at each end (fig. 44), occur in cornelian and agate, onyx, quartz, amethyst and jasper and in blue, green, red and whitish glass; some of the glass cones are ornamented with little strips of mosaic. It is very rare to find one of these collared beads outside India, though why they were not exported is a mystery.

(f) *Moulded beads.* Several beads are found in the forms of cornerless cubes and truncated hexagonal bicones, the latter forms being nearly always of « Indian red » glass (see below).

Most of these special forms of beads are ancient, belonging to the first millennium B.C. Many may be ascribed to the 7th or 6th century B.C., most will abound about 300 B.C. and the collared beads were probably still made at the beginning of our era. It is only then that drawn beads begin to conquer the market, as they can be made in series of dozens and hundreds, while the wound beads have to be made individually by hand. It is a very interesting fact that the common wound bead, the simplest of all, was made in India only in negligible quantities, if at all. We will see below that when trade grows in the Indian Ocean during the first centuries of our era, multiple-wound beads at first play a role, but by the beginning of the 6th century A.D. the drawn cylinder beads take over, and in the 9th century the spherical and lenticular multiple wound beads disappear.

In the Bahmani period in India, between A.D. 1200 and 1400, virtually no beads other than drawn ones are found.

Modern Indian beads, such as those from the large factory in Purdalpur, are wound and moulded in rather primitive ways.

One last remark. One colour prevails in Indian beads, the so-called « Indian red », caused by very small crystals of copper oxide. In hydrated form this may even give an orange colour, which is rare in the west, but occurs eastward as far as Indian beads go. Only in the last thirty years has this dull, opaque Indian red tended to disappear, together with the old method of colouring glass a beautiful wine red by means of gold. The shining red colour of to-day is caused by selenium.

CHAPTER VII

Beads from the East African Coast

A. ZANZIBAR (van der Sleen, 1956)

The beautiful, shady island of Zanzibar with its unlimited supply of splendid, clear fresh water has been a mart for at least the last 2000 years, perhaps for much longer (Schoff, 1912). There are other marts, nearly as old and perhaps older than Zanzibar, for instance Arikamedu (Wheeler, 1946) near Pondicherry and Kuala Selinsing (Beck, 1930) in Perak. We may be sure that others will soon be discovered (cf. Chau Yu Kua; Hirth and Rockhill, 1911). One way to find out about these old marts, and their connexions, is the study of beads, although coins, pottery (china if you like), inscriptions and so on may be of equal or greater help.

When east African beads first awakened my interest, being so different from the beads that are worn nowadays in the heart of Africa, I thought about the possibility of their having been imported from Egypt, the nearest place where beads were abundant in tombs and excavations. So I studied Egyptian beads in the museums of London, Oxford and Cambridge, but found none comparable with the east African trade-wind beads, and the Director of the Cairo Museum, to whom I sent some, said that he had never seen any like them. It seems very strange that bead types, which are found all over east Africa and southern India and even as far east as Japan (Ueno Museum, Tokyo), should never have moved up the Red Sea to Egypt.

The first information I obtained on this question came from an unexpected quarter. Mr. Alan Villiers, an officer in the English merchant navy, who sailed the replica of the Mayflower to America, travelled with an Arabian dhow from Kuwait on the Persian Gulf to Zanzibar and wrote a very interesting book about his trip (Villiers, 1934). He describes an impromptu talk given by the captain of the dhow to a gathering on board, one quiet summer night. The captain said how good Allah is to the true believers. How Allah made the fearful, dry desert, to keep the people of the western world out of the Indian Ocean : east and west the desert, south the roaring winds and terrific waves, that rendered travelling south of Zanzibar practically impossible and then, last but not least, the terrible

Red Sea, with its rocks and reefs and never changing head-winds. « All these are ways of Allah the merciful to keep the Indian Ocean for the Arabs and nobody else. »

All this, of course, is not quite true. More than 4000 years ago there was a lively trade between India and the Mesopotamian civilization, and when Egypt became a world power the riches of the east came via Babylon to the Mediterranean. Before the beginning of our era the Dravidians already sailed the Indian Ocean, visiting the Gulf of Aden and moving on along the east coast of Africa (Renou and Filiozat, 1947). The Arabs gave them a free hand, but kept for themselves the rich trade in muslins, precious stones, spices and incense with Egypt. On Sokotra and near Cape Gardafui were the ports to which the Arabs brought the Indian wares, and often brought them thence overland to the upper Nile. That the route from Egypt through the Red Sea to the land of Punt in Somaliland, the Opone of the Periplus (Schoff, 1912), was dangerous, was proved by the fact that expeditions from Egypt only went there during the 11th, 12th and 18th dynasties (Huntingford, 1950). It was only after Rome had conquered Egypt that Roman and Greek merchants could establish factories in India (e.g. Arikamedu; Wheeler, 1946), thanks to the discovery of the monsoon winds by Hippalos (Pliny, N.H., VI, 26) before or during the early 1st century A.D. [1] This trade lasted only a few centuries till Byzantium took the place of Rome and re-established the old route via the Persian Gulf. After that the Mohammedans put an iron curtain across Egypt and north Africa and the Indian and Arab sailors could trade again as masters from Madagascar to Japan. The Indian trade-wind beads resumed their task all over the Indian Ocean until the products of European industry, and money, changed the whole aspect of trade in the eastern seas (Hourani, 1951).

It is of interest that some Egyptian and Syrian beads and other glassware found their way overland along the silk route to China and Japan. I have not yet discovered whether the Chinese or the Japanese ever made glass beads for barter abroad.

We may divide the Zanzibar beads into six groups :
1. Stone beads.
2. Multiple-wound beads of opaque glass.
3. Drawn beads of opaque glass.
4. Spirally wound beads of glass.

---

[1] WHEELER, Sir Mortimer (1954), pp. 126 ff.

5. Modern European beads.
6. Shell beads.

1. *Stone beads.*

The oldest beads were made out of semi-precious or ornamental stones or minerals, and perhaps some from shell also. The best known and most widely found are those of cornelian, agate, quartz and amethyst. Such material must have been very hard for ancient men to work and so the beads were very expensive. The first imitations must have been the so-called faience beads of Egypt and Mesopotamia, which were current from before 3000 B.C. to the beginning of our era. It is very important to remember that no faience beads have ever been found in east Africa. This makes it fairly certain that between 3000 B.C. and A.D. 1000 there can have been very little trade between east Africa and Egypt.

2. *Multiple-wound beads of opaque glass.*

All the beads found in east African coastal settlements, which belong to times before the arrival of the Portuguese, must have been brought in by Arabs, Persians, Indians and Chinese, coming to east Africa, as they still do, by the aid of the monsoon winds. These enabled vessels to sail in an easy, though often dangerous, way southward during the European winter and to return north-eastwards between June and September. Is it not a nice idea to imagine that one is handling beads which may have been the prototypes of Sindbad the Sailor's cargo of money-bags, when he went exploring the coast of the Indian Ocean? I like to call them trade-wind beads and I wish that Scheherazade had told us, in *The Arabian Nights*, where they got the specimens which they took to barter with the natives they met in Java and Sumatra and, after repassing India and Pakistan, to continue this barter on the east coast of Africa and in the flourishing towns of Malindi, Zanzibar, Tanga, Kilwa, Dar es Salaam and Sofala.

The beads that belong to this group are by far the oldest glass beads from the east African coast. The workmen who made them knew how to make red, yellow, green, blue and black opaque glass. They knew how to draw a lump of semi-molten glass into a thin rod, but their lamps were not hot enough to melt rods thicker than a few millimetres evenly. They knew how to give the beads other forms by pressing the viscous material in moulds or between metal plates, but again, their fires were not hot enough to remove the traces of their inadequate methods of fabrication.

In Zanzibar and around other old Arab towns globular (fig. 45) and lenticular (fig. 46) beads are found, where the process of making the beads from thin rods is plainly visible, yet these little channels and markings disappear as soon as the bead is turned a few times in a somewhat hotter flame. Hunter found a few in a 15th-century tomb near Dar es Salaam and Kirkman found them under a tomb, dated 1399 (Kirkman, 1954).

There are two main varieties of these beads, globular and oval, the latter sometimes developing into long biconicals and very flat lenticular beads, that might be called very short biconicals, with a nearly flat base. Both types are nearly always made in opaque glass, either black (coloured by iron), Indian red (by copper oxide), yellow (by chrome), blue (by cobalt) and bluish green (by copper). I know only one green and two blue beads of clear transparent glass.

All these beads have a tapering perforation, in which they differ from Egyptian short biconical beads, where the perforation is equally wide at both one ends. Such beads, wound from thin rods, are very rare in European museums.

I know only one necklace of black globular multiple-wound beads in the Victoria and Albert Museum and one of similar green beads in the Rhodesian National Museum, found in the ruins of Zimbabwe. The British Museum possesses a few globular beads from Zanzibar, Pemba and Kilwa, varying in size from 18 to 5 mm. diameter. The black ones are by far the largest.

The second variety of opaque-coloured multiple-wound glass beads I have called lenticulars. Sometimes they look almost discoid. I should like to call them the « guide-beads » of the trade winds. The form is infrequent. I know beads of the same form only from Egypt in the 18th dynasty, about 1400 B.C., but then they are generally not made of glass but of cornelian, lapis lazuli, quartz, steatite, etc. : such beads occur on the famous earrings of Tutankhamun. Other small bicones were found in the ruins of Roman settlements on the Rhine during the migration period (A.D. 400 to 600). The form may also be found in gold in Mohenjodaro and in amber in northern Europe. Those on the Rhine were cobalt-blue glass.

There is, however, one place from where multiple-wound beads, the globular as well as the lenticular ones of opaque glass, comparable with those found in east Africa, are recorded. That is Kolhapur in Bombay state, where the site of an old town, Brahmapuri, has been excavated by Sankalia and Dikshit (1952). The excavation proved that

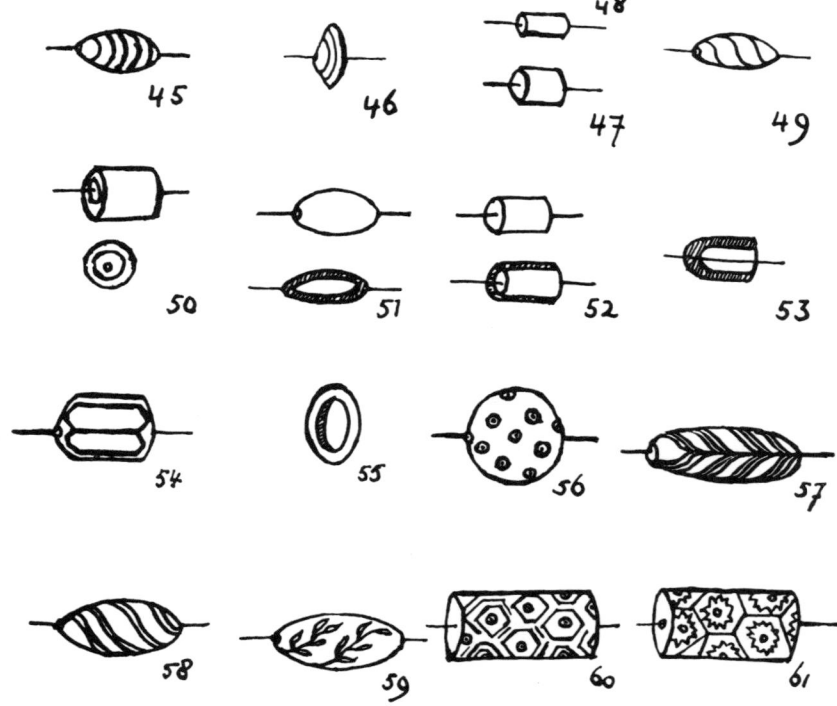

PLATE IV, figs. 45-61

Beads from Zanzibar.
45 to 48. Trade-wind beads.
49 to 61. Later beads from Venice or Gablonz.

the glass must have been made locally and, as the excavation was done with great care, we know that most of the lenticular beads were made and used during the Satavahana or Andhra period, 2nd century B.C. to 2nd century A.D. These beads may have been brought to Zanzibar by the first Dravidian or Persian ships that ever anchored on this coast (Renou, 1947).

Many multiple-wound beads of globular form and a few lenticular ones, all *c.* 12 mm. long, have been found in the ruins of Zimbabwe (Caton Thomson, 1931) and a few globular beads in the fortress of Mapungubwe in the northern Transvaal (Fouché, 1957). Drawn beads of opaque glass also occur at Zimbabwe.

It is very interesting to note that the common, simple, wound beads, made by winding a half-molten rod of glass once around the wire, and than cutting off, are not found on sites in east Africa before Portuguese times. They were made in the 14th century B.C. at Tell el Amarna and later in Egypt and throughout the Mediterranean, but, as far as I know, they do not occur in India, either, before the 16th century A.D. After that time Venice and other European factories sent millions of them all over the world.

3. *Drawn beads of opaque glass.*

Drawn beads form by far the greater part of all the older beads that are picked up or excavated on the sea-shore or near ruins in east Africa. The first drawn beads appear in Egypt between the 1st century B.C. and the 2nd century A.D. It is generally clear that these must have been partly severed in a semi-fluid state and then broken off after cooling. Later, drawn beads were separated only when the glass had quite solidified. They were then broken or hacked from the tube, exactly as happens nowadays in Murano near Venice (Pasquato and Morazzoni, 1953). These opaque drawn beads (fig. 47 and 48) occur in very great quantities, in the same colours, and of the same constitution as the opaque multiple-wound beads (group 2). The glass of the « black » beads is dark brown instead of green, but it is again caused by iron. The shape of the drawn beads is generally cylindrical, but often becomes oblate, by re-melting, scouring or wear. Very often drawn beads can be recognized from stripes or series of small air-bubbles that are visible parallel to the perforation. When semi-transparent, the colours are of a strange bluish green, different from the trade-beads of today.

We know from historical records that, when the Portuguese first came to the east African coast, the natives would not exchange their gold and ivory for the beads they had brought from Europe (Theal, 1898) and the Portuguese were obliged to fetch from the shores of India (Negapatnam) shiploads of the same kinds of beads as the Arabs used for barter. These drawn beads must therefore have been in use during the first decades of the 16th century. The old Portuguese writers, according to Stanley (1866), described these beads as « *barros miudas* », which is said to mean « earthenware beads ». This may seem strange, but the Indian-red beads, in particular, coloured as they are with cuprous oxide, really look very much like red pottery.

Modern authors have introduced the unfortunate term « paste », whereas the beads are nothing but opaque glass. It is interesting that powder from these Indian-red beads under the microscope, as well as to the naked eye, is grey and transparent when studied by transmitted light with the powder held between two slide-glasses. When light is reflected from the powder, the beautiful red colour is visible.

These drawn beads, which are from 1 to 10 mm. long and 1 1/2 to 12 mm. in diameter, form the great mass of beads found not only in eastern Africa, on sites such as Zanzibar and Kilwa Kisiwani (personal observation), Malindi (Kirkman, 1954) and others, but also in Java (personal observation), Sumatra (van der Hoop, 1932, in stone-slab graves), Malaysia (Perak, Kuala Selinsing and Johore : Gardner, 1932, and Beck, 1930). We meet them again in Madagascar (p.56 and p.88), in the Ueno Museum in Tokyo, and in the Bahmani layers in Kolhapur (Brahmapuri ; Sankalia and Dikshit, 1952, and letters). In this last place they are considered to be 12th to 14th century, while in the others, if dated, they belong to the 8th-century deposits and may be even earlier.

4. *Spirally-wound beads of glass* (fig. 49).

I think, that here is the best place to mention the modern beads that were imported after the 16th century into eastern and southern Africa.

On all the explored sites in Zanzibar, Kenya, Tanzania, etc., we find a few ellipsoid spirally-wound beads, made of semi-transparent glass. Their colours differ from those of the trade-wind beads, being pink, green, orange, blue (which is rare) and opaque white (which in some places form the greater quantity). Some of these beads are unusually large. The normal size is 8 to 10 mm. long and 5 to 6 mm. in diameter. The large beads were found in Zanzibar. All these beads may be of considerable age, except the opaque white ones, which were still in use round Lake Nyasa and were used by the White Fathers when, about 1900, they first penetrated so far into the heart of Africa.

These ellipsoid spirally-wound beads will probably have been among the first beads imported from outside the Indian Ocean, perhaps by the Portuguese, but as yet I have no proof of this.

The Portuguese power in east Africa did not last very long because, amongst other reasons, the expected gains from the gold trade did not materialize. When the Dutch were building up their colonial empire in the east, one of the Portuguese factories they conquered was Negapatnam, which fell into their hands in 1660. The import of the trade-wind beads must have stopped shortly afterwards. Still, trade went on and so the Portuguese and other traders along the coast must have found other kinds of beads to use to buy gold, ivory and slaves.

5. *Modern European beads.*

It seems reasonable to suppose that the Portuguese and other skippers of the Indian Ocean looked to Europe for materials to use in bartering. They had already been importing beads into Angola for more than 150 years and must have brought the European beads, which they used there, to the east coast as well. Now most of the Angola beads consisted of small narrow glass tubes, which the old records describe as small beads from Flanders (Sparmann, 1785; Wikar, 1799). However, as far as I know beads were never made in Flanders, but were probably imported there from Venice. These short cylinder beads are still known in South Africa and from there they spread to the Orange River as well as to the Limpopo. We may take the old sacred beads of the Venda, the so-called « beads of the water » (van Riet Lowe, 1937) as an example. These are found only rarely on the east African coast. They are still the proud possessions of the Venda, the inhabitants of the Zoutpansbergen, a high mountain range in north-eastern Transvaal. These and other kinds of glass beads came to South Africa in such great quantities that Johan van Riebeeck, the founder of the Dutch colony of the Cape of Good Hope in 1651, had to order brass beads from Java because the Hottentots were satiated with glass beads, so that they would not take them in payment for their cattle. It is interesting to note here, in passing, that as early as the 18th century the Portuguese were bringing wares overland from Loango in Angola to Tete on the Zambesi.

About the end of the 17th and beginning of the 18th century we find another kind of bead on the coast and also inland, in much greater quantities than before. These were much larger than the small tubulars of Angola, being cylinder beads, also drawn but up to 10 mm. in length and diameter and hardly ever smaller than 5 mm. They are mostly of two types : white opaque cylinders that sometimes show crackled surfaces, and Indian-red beads that derive their colour from a very thin coating of the surface, the greater part of the bead being dark or light green, brown or even blue (fig. 53). These beads are often very irregular in form and shade of colour and differ greatly from the modern beads of the same type. The small red-on-green beads of 2 by 4 mm. length and diameter are certainly European of the end of the 18th century and come in with a later variety, the hexagonal blues and the red-on-white or yellow, where we again have to distinguish between drawn and wound beads.

The large white and the red-on-green beads are found in Rhodesia (Schofield, 1943) in great quantities in the so-called « hoards » of chiefs, who had to flee their country and thought to save their treasures by burying them under the floors of their huts, or in caves and rock-shelters. The Selukwe and Penhalonga hoards are well known; both are now in the museum in Bulawayo and I know a third find from Headlands not far from Umtali, all in Rhodesia (personal observation). These hoards date from the beginning of the 19th century. Big white cylindrical beads with a greenish tinge were still used by the Missionary Expedition of 1902 in Rhodesia.

The Indian red-on-green beads are still worn by most women in Rhodesia, where they are called « spirit beads », because they are said to contain the spirits of ancestors. They are mostly worn under the clothes round the belly and each woman gives one or two to each of her daughters. Both the white and the red-on-green beads are regularly found on the coast at Zanzibar, Dar es Salaam, Kilwa and Sofala, but generally in small numbers. A large red-on-green bead is illustrated in colour by Caton Thompson (1931, colour plate 6*b*).

The large white beads are probably the first white beads that came to Africa south of the equator. Dapper (1676) says that white beads were first imported into Africa about 1660; and, certainly, no beads of this colour were found in the ruins of Zimbabwe, Khami, etc.; not even in Mapungubwe, except of course the shell beads, which I shall mention later.

At the end of the 18th century two other types of beads came into use in Zambia and Rhodesia (personal observation). Both are transparent red-on-white. One is a thick cylindrical drawn bead of about 10 by 12 mm., consisting of a narrow transparent red coat over a thick opaque white kernel (fig. 50), from which it acquired the name of « ox-eye bead ». Smaller examples down to 5 by 5 mm. also occur, with the interior cylinder sometimes pink or yellow (fig. 52).

The second type is also transparent red outside and has a rather narrow white kernel (fig. 51), which is hardly visible at the outside. These are big, wound beads, oval or globular, up to 15 by 15 mm. Air bubbles several mm. long generally visible to the naked eye, lying perpendicular to the perforation, prove that they are wound beads. I have the impression that these two types of red-on-white beads were not fashionable for long. The longer, ellipsoid wound form of red over narrow white was worn mostly by men and then only in ceremonial attire, with perhaps a large shell bead as a pendant. These shiny red-on-white beads are called « cornaline d'Aleppo » in U.S.A.

The beginning of the 19th century quite certainly brought Venetian beads in ever growing quantities. One of the first, perhaps, was a bead imported into Tanzania and from there to Zambia and the Congo by the slave traders. It is a large semi-opaque, greyish-white bead in the form of a short, drawn cylinder, 12 to 15 mm. long and 20 mm. wide. The price of a slave was a girdle of such beads corresponding to the circumference of his belly.

With, or shortly after, these large beads came the well-known blue, wound annulars (fig. 55) of 4 by 12 mm. and the equally well-known cornerless dark blue, drawn, hexagonal beads, that were still in use by some tribes in 1910. The annulars were worn by chiefs who met Livingstone at Victoria Falls. The hexagonals were known by the Rhodesians as ambassador beads, since they were given by the chiefs to witch-doctors, who were sent, high into the Matopo Hills, to ask advice from the great god of the Matabele.

Another newcomer in south, east and central Africa at about the same time was a large globular bead of about 12 to 15 mm. diameter. It appeared in transparent as well as in opaque glass, was always wound and decorated with white lines or red, white or black spots. They could be had in white, transparent red, green and blue and, later, mostly in black with white spots (fig. 56).

A milk-white bead with small blue spots was in great demand when the railway was building in Rhodesia (1900-1902) and therefore was called the traina bead. Elsewhere they were called Birmingham beads because the English used them for buying palm-oil.

In the north and east large ornamented beads, like the palm-leaf type (fig. 57) and barrels with spiral design (fig. 58), were brought in by the slave-traders and remained fashionable until well into the 20th century. At the same time, south of the Limpopo, beadwork (fig. 62,

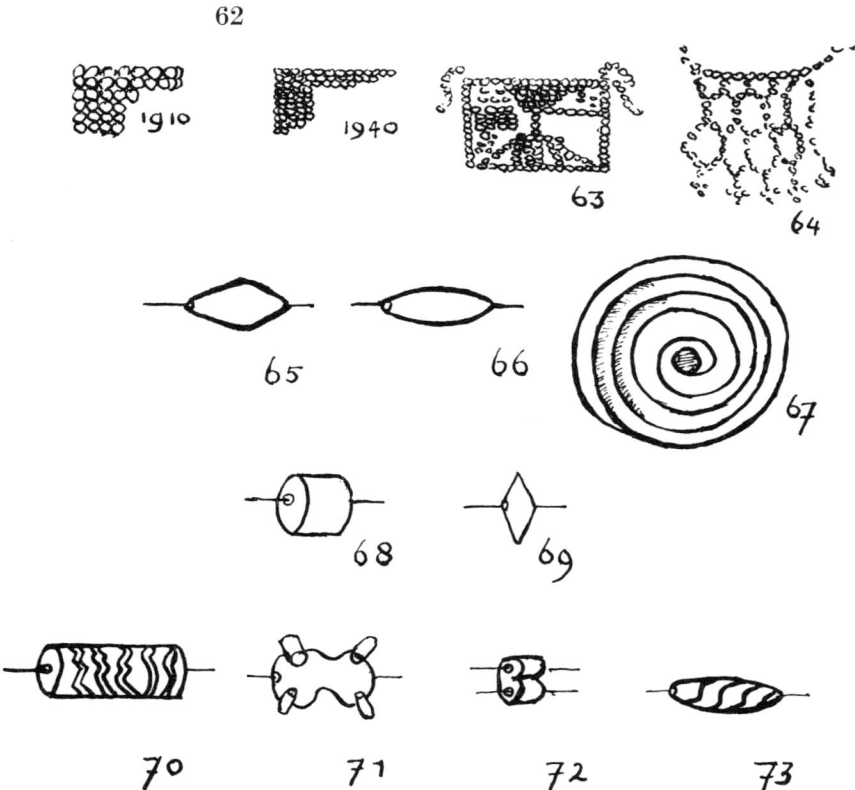

PLATE V, figs. 62-73
Some forms of modern beads.

63, 64) came into fashion, straps and aprons being decorated with geometrical figures of different coloured small beads, which were made, e.g., into love-letters and all kind of necklaces and collars.

The last change in bead-fashion in Africa occurred some twenty years ago, when the pressed plastic and porcelain beads of Herzogenrath (fig. 68), Gablonz and Briare conquered many markets, becoming specially popular because they are pressed in moulds, are absolutely regular and are all exactly the same size, a feature the natives always greatly liked. It is interesting to see how, in different parts of Africa, different forms are wanted, forms that frequently are imitations of very ancient beads.

6. *Shell beads* (fig. 65, 66, 67).

In the old days, as we shall see (p.87-88), shell beads must have been manufactured in Kilwa Kisiwani on the coast of Tanzania These are usually small or large cylinders, from 12 mm. to 100 mm. long, often cigar-shaped. The biconical form is often found too, and these are often so large, being standard beads of 37 mm., that they can have been made only from the giant clam shell, *Tridacna gigas*. The larger cylinders are called chimanda in east Africa. Other old shell beads have a much wider range, for instance the Ndoro or Mpande (local names), which are discs 25 to 50 mm. in diameter with a beautiful spiral groove, since it is the top of a large Conus-shell (*C. betulina*, *virgo*, *literata*, *marmorata*, etc. : Quiggin, 1949). These discs are often worn as pendants and have been found in the Zimbabwe ruins, and all along the coast as well as inland, e.g. in Bechuanaland and Uganda, but you will meet them just as frequently in Celebes and the Moluccas. A hundred years ago two of these pendants bought a cow, one a woman in Zambia. Nowadays, instead, you may collect specimens made of white porcelain or shining red plastic.

Much better known and more frequent are small disc beads, cut from pieces of ostrich-egg shell, that were already made in Sumerian times at Ur, as well as by the Bushmen, when they still roamed free all over Africa. They are still made both by Bantu and Bushmen. The size varies from 3 mm. to 12 mm. They are generally very nicely rounded, well shaped by long tedious work. Easier to fashion are imitations made from the shell of a huge land snail (*Achatina sp.*) and sometimes from a bivalve (*Unio sp.*).

B. KILWA KISIWANI

About 200 miles south of Zanzibar another, much smaller island or, better, a peninsula, called Kilwa Kisiwani, lies off the east African coast. Arab and Portuguese writers like Ibn Batuta, Vasco da Gama and d'Almeida tell us about a town of several thousand inhabitants and left information in a Chronicle of Kilwa that led to excavations by the Revd. Dr. Gervase Mathew (*Man*, 1956, n° 61). In medieval times Kilwa had its own mint, but before that thousands of beads must have been used there, as we find them now strewn over the beaches. Practically all of them are trade-wind beads, such as I have described from Zanzibar, but with one rather important difference. In Zanzibar amongst a hundred beads there will always be a number of multiple-wound ones; in Kilwa, only one in every thousand is one of these old-fashioned specimens. We could expect this, because the Kilwa Chronicle tells us that the town was not founded until A.D. 925, while Zanzibar was already known at the beginning of our era. The old-fashioned multiple-wound beads had disappeared long before the 10th century, because of the monsoon trade. Typical at Kilwa are quantities of limestone beads, many of which are probably made from large Tridacna shells.

C. MALINDI

Malindi and the island of Lamu about 200 miles north of Zanzibar are known to be very old settlements. Near Malindi, which is developing now as a seaside resort, Kirkman conducted important excavations in what he calls « The Arab City of Gedi » (Kirkman, 1954). He found, of course, many beads. Regrettably, he does not distinguish between wound and drawn beads, but his illustrations and descriptions allow us to recognize the trade-wind beads. We must, also, substitute the term « opaque glass » where he speaks of « paste » and « cane ». Very important is his recognition of pre-mosque levels and specially the beads, found under the dated tomb of 1399.

Kirkman mentions limestone beads of local make and a few large ostrich-egg shell beads.

All over the East African coast from Mogadishu to Sofala the trade-wind beads can be found at nearly every small port which was used by the Arabs in the gold and ivory and slave trade, first behind the backs of the Portuguese, and later, when the English began their fight against slavery.

D. MADAGASCAR

The Great Island, as the Malagasy people like it to be called, has a bead-literature all of its own. It began when Millot (1952) wrote about trade in the Indian Ocean and said he had found there beads of intricate form and beautiful colours. At the same time Fourneau (1952) had just announced that similar ones had been found in the middle Congo. In 1955 Professor Millot sent me several thousand beads which he had excavated near Vohémar, a ruined village destroyed by the Portuguese during their first landing on the island. So the beads and other objects should all date from before the Portuguese arrival. My report on them never reached the Institute at Tananarive, but the following is an extract from it :

a. Cornelian beads, hexagonal cylinders 25 mm. long. Many dozens.
b. Cornelian beads in lozenge form. Two dozen.
c. Cornelian beads in lozenge form with three perforations. Spacer-beads.
d. Cornelian globular beads. A few hundreds.
e. Cornelian hexagonal short bicones. Two dozen.
f. Quartz globular beads. Two dozen.
g. Quartz hexagonal short bicones. Half a dozen.
h. Opaque glass beads, Indian-red, drawn, of half the normal size (3 mm.). A thousand.
i. Opaque glass beads, green, drawn, small. A thousand.
j. Opaque glass beads, yellow, drawn, small. Seven to eight hundred.
k. Opaque glass beads, dark blue, drawn, small. Seven to eight hundred.
l. Square cylindrical glass beads, blue-on-white. A few dozen.
m. Chevron or star beads, small, up to 10 mm. About fifty.
n. Somewhat larger opaque glass beads of the normal size of trade-wind beads (6-10 mm.) but no blues amongst them. A few dozen.

There are four remarkable things about this list :

1) There is a very large quantity of beautiful, polished cornelian beads in this cemetery, nearly all orange-red.
2) There is an extraordinary quantity of specially small trade-wind beads, the typical opaque beads of Indian make.
3) There are the small blue opaque drawn trade-wind beads which I had never seen before. There must have been a certain dislike of dark blue beads along the east coast of Africa. Was it perhaps a colour of mourning or something like that for some tribes ?
4) All the beads from a to k were made in India : those under l and m were not, but were probably made in Holland in the middle of the 17th century.

Now it is curious that I found more of these Dutch beads in Nîmes in southern France than I found in Vohémar. It was known that about 1904 a postmaster named Maurein had collected much material out of graves in Vohémar and that he was repatriated to France and brought his collection with him. Visiting the museum in Nîmes on a rainy day, I saw displayed a series of necklaces, which I recognized instantly as old Malagasy material. The curator was kind enough to let me take colour pictures of the beads and then asked me if I was not interested in the other finds from Vohémar. And there they were ! First, Chinese dishes of the 12th and 13th centuries, bronze and silver and iron work, stone pipkins on three legs such as are so well known from China in bronze, but here made locally from a chloritoschist. What interested me most was a set of bronze mirrors with designs and what we thought would be Arab script. None of our Arabic scholars in Leyden, however, could help me to decipher them. Nîmes is a lot nearer than Madagascar and I hope some young linguist will take the hint and go there to help in solving the riddle of this script. I am sure he will get all possible help from the people in Tananarive and in Nîmes. He can find my note about Nîmes in *Le Naturaliste Malgache*, XII (van der Sleen, 1960).

A lot more has been done in Madagascar about beads, however. In 1960 Mrs Solange Bernard Thierry (see bibliography) published an article about « The magic beads of Madagascar ». She studied all the beads that were available in the markets in Tananarive and other towns and bought with the beads the tale of what they are good for. Beads from Venice and Gablonz, etc., are sold by the Arab traders as medicine for any thing you want to cure ! It might be worth doing the same work in other parts of Africa, because this knowledge (?) — such as it is — is disappearing quickly. Her next publication (Thierry, 1961) is of much more value, as she gives a summary of all the beads excavated in Madagascar, with interesting illustrations. It was not yet known, however, in Madagascar that I had shown that all the trade-wind beads, the very small ones as well as those of normal size, had been made in India.

The cemetery at Vohémar offered a very valuable chance to study the inhabitants who lived in the island before the 16th century. Anthropological studies showed that amongst the Arabs and negroes there were quite a number of mongoloid, or perhaps better Polynesian and Indonesian, perhaps Malay, types. This coincides very well with the fact that several cultural objects, as for instance the outrigger canoe, the whole of the wet rice culture, and several words in the Malagasian language point at contacts with, perhaps even immigration from, Java. It is quite possible that the cornelians as well as the small trade-wind beads came direct to Madagascar across the Indian Ocean with equatorial currents. There is much more to learn on the Great Island.

E. SOFALA

Sofala was an important and well-known port in Portuguese times, It is known, too, that there were two ports, one in the mouth of the river, where the Portuguese used to land, and another one on a sand bar just north of the river, where the Arab ships struck shore. The Arab port left no traces except for a few trade-wind beads that could be picked up there some 50 years ago. From the Portuguese harbour-works some huge blocks of masonry were still visible in 1955, but we met an old Arab there who had been at school in rooms of the fortress some 60 years ago. He knew that piles of Chinese plates had been left there in the cellars. As happens all over the world, the river had silted up and then changed its course, so that shipping has changed too, and now uses the port of Beira. We visited Sofala, using a small plane that went twice a week to pick up fish for the town of Beira from the small fishing villages along the coast. Where old Sofala harbour was you will find only modern beads, perhaps a hundred years old, such as the red-on-green cylinders and the omnipresent blue annulars.

CHAPTER VIII

Beads from the Rhodesian Ruins

The importance of towns like Sofala, Beira, Zanzibar, Kilwa, Bagamoyo, etc., lay in the fact that from all of them trails went inland, and were used by the people from central Africa to bring first ivory, then gold and, later, slaves to the coast. Here all this merchandise could be sold, or rather bartered, for much higher prices in cotton, different kinds of beads and shell money. Portuguese travellers including many priests used these trails to go inland in search of more gold and ivory and left us very readable accounts of their adventures. They were not expert writers and you can not trust every word they wrote, but they were the only writers of history in those days. They exaggerated much about kings and palaces of Monomotapa and the gold mines, but now that travellers, and specially archaeologists, have unearthed Zimbabwe and Nanantali, Dhlo-Dhlo and Mapungubwe, we can better understand the wonder of the poor priests and soldiers, coming to large open places and groups of buildings they had not expected to find in the land of small straw huts and jungle paths, only reached after months of travel under very unpleasant circumstances.

Zimbabwe is a fortified hill on top of which are rooms and corridors and open squares of all kinds, difficult of access, easy to defend; and just below these there is an elliptical area surrounded by a double wall of granite slabs up to 9 m. high.

In 1931 Miss G. Caton Thomson, after six months of exploring and excavating not only Zimbabwe, but many other ruined sites also, published a book entitled *The Zimbabwe Culture*. Combining her results with other, earlier attempts to understand the lie of the land and the purpose of the remains, the conclusion had to be that Zimbabwe was the centre and capital of a large part of central Africa. Here ivory and gold were won and exported to the east coast along a line formed by a series of stone buildings or fortifications, each about a day's journey from the next one. The beads, that were often paid for with their own weight in gold, were unearthed in large quantities and show that Zimbabwe must already have had connexions with the coast and in this way with India, long before the trade-wind beads changed from multiple-wound to the cheaper drawn ones, a change which took place between the 8th and 10th centuries of our era. The building of the structures we now see probably took place between the 10th and the 12th centuries. When the Portuguese arrived decadence must already have set in.

In the frontispiece of Miss Caton Thompson's book the beads numbered 4 and 5 are mostly multiple-wound beads, specially 4 *i*, 4 *h* and 5 *c*. Unfortunately the beads illustrated on plates XLV, XLVI and XLVII are now lost, but Miss Caton Thompson recognized these types of beads immediately in my collection. This was just 25 years after the appearance of her book in which H.C. Beck (Caton Thompson, 1931, p. 229) pointed out the similarity of these beads to some specimens found in India. This caused me to have a good look at Indian literature, where I found publications by Prof. M. G. Dikshit (1952). We corresponded; and later I visited him in Rampur, saw his own collections and many others, and gathered material for chemical analyses : for such analysis was the only way to prove that there was not only a superficial likeness between the Indian and African beads, but that they were identical.

I am, thus, able to present here a few analyses made by the Stazione Sperimentale del Vetro in Murano (Tornati and van der Sleen, 1960).

The following analyses show that the old multiple-wound beads have the same chemical composition as the drawn beads which are 1000 years younger. All the beads were collected in Zanzibar.

ANALYSES OF BEADS FROM ZANZIBAR

	MULTIPLE-WOUND BEADS A.D. 200-800				DRAWN BEADS A.D. 800-1600	
	Red	Yellow	Yellow	Green	Red	Blue-green
SiO_2	61,91	58,00	58,94	61,23	60,65	63,90
Fe_2O_3	3,91	1,308	1,05	1,76	3,56	0,449
TiO_2	0,33	0,34	0,245	0,326	0,36	0,147
Al_2O_3	9,08	9,04	5,79	8,18	5,70	5,13
CaO	3,50	2,30	5,40	3,07	5,20	4,71
MgO	1,18	0,94	3,27	0,71	2,49	4,11
Na_2O	16,03	18,40	15,80	18,02	17,80	17,18
K_2O	3,25	2,86	5,59	3,46	1,84	2,79
Cu_2O	0,38	—	—	—	0,70	—
SnO_2	trace	3,28	2,80	1,91	—	—
P_2O_5	0,43	3,35	0,47	0,109	0,38	—
MNO	0,055	—	0,45	0,59	0,08	—
So_3	—	0,10	0,13	—	—	0,31
Cr_2O_3	—	—	—	—	0,0032	—
CuO	—	—	—	0.718	—	0,81
FeO	—	—	—	—	—	0,293
PbO	—	—	—	—	—	—

The differences between these analyses lie mostly in small quantities of colouring matter like copper, chrome and iron oxides. There is, however, some phosphoric acid in each of the beads, which is seldom found in ancient glass. It occurs in most Indian beads, as we can see in the following analyses, which I include for comparison with the above :

ANALYSES OF BEADS FROM INDIA

	BEADS FROM ARIKAMEDU A.D. 1 to 200		BEADS FROM KAUSAMBI 200 B.C. to A.D. 200		
	Red Drawn	Green Drawn	Green Wound	Blue Wound	Orange Drawn
SiO_2	64,810	75,90	65,08	76,42	57,34
Fe_2O_3	1,205	2,584	1,122	1,187	4,48
TiO_2	0,311	0,163	0,2929	0,105	0,38
Al_2O_3	3,41	2,88	4,02	2,39	4,70
CaO	4,81	1,84	2,23	3,14	3,30
MgO	2,25	1,31	1,69	0,55	2,81
Na_2O	11,35	4,27	13,57	4,11	7,50
Ka_2O	4,32	3,93	2,92	10,12	6,89
Cu_2O	1,333	—	—	—	10,89
SnO_2	0,39	0,63	1,84	—	—
P_2O_5	5,00	4,81	5,16	0,10	1,95
MnO	—	—	—	1,42	0,39
SO_3	0,10	0,20	0,25	—	—
Cr_2O_3	—	—	—	—	—
CuO	0,721	1,50	1,803	0,284	—
FeO	—	—	—	—	—
PbO	—	—	—	—	—

These analyses show the composition of five Indian-made beads from find-spots in out-of-the-way places in India; first the Romano-Indian trading-post of Arikamedu near Pondicherry, and second a rich ancient town in central India. As there is difference in place and time, there will be differences in chemical composition too. However, if we study these analyses with others that have already been published, e.g. those by Dikshit from Tripuri (1955), by Lal (1953) and by Van der Hoop (1932) we have enough material for comparison with the trade-wind beads.

Farther south in Africa beads are very rarely found on the coast except perhaps some cornelians in the form of raw material, roughly shaped in lozenge or biconical forms, still needing chipping, grinding and polishing. I have already pointed out (p. 76) that between Zanzibar and the Cape the ships nearly always have to fight heavy head-winds and rough seas.

Every archaeologist should read C.R. Boxer, *Tragic History of the Sea*, 1598-1622 (1959) to get an idea of the overloaded ships with hundreds of passengers and know how many of these « carhavellos » were shipwrecked on this inhospitable coast. In the 17th century many ships of the East India Company sailed from Gujerat and Broach to round the Cape and, although generally better equipped than the Portuguese fleet, several of these, also, foundered within sight of the coast of Natal.

The cargo-lists of these ships are easily accessible in the State-Archives in The Hague. They include many boxes filled with little stones of Cambay, roughly chipped in certain forms that could be ground and polished and beautified by the Dutch jewellers and coral-grinders.

*
* *

We have seen, now, that the Indian-made trade-wind beads played a very important role in the traffic, commerce and barter all along the east coast and even far inland in central Africa. It is very improbable that trade and commerce should not just as well have gone northward and eastward from the old Indian ports. We know that Dutch as well as Portuguese merchantmen on the east African coast met not only Arabs but ships from southern India and even Chinese junks as well. So we must visit famous marts in Malacca, Java, Sumatra and indeed all the important harbours in Indonesia, and onwards also into China and Japan, in our next chapter.

CHAPTER IX

Beads from the Indian Ocean and farther east

As far as I know, no collectors or excavators have worked in Mogadishu or Aden. In Aden there are a few well-known collections of beads, but they are more of interest to a jeweller than to an archaeologist, since they include almost nothing but agates and cornelians.

About Broach and Gujerat, the harbours whence tons of « stones » from Cambay and other towns and factories have been shipped away, no investigations are known to me, although there begins the long range of ports that traded all over the Indian coast using the trade-wind beads which I have described from Zanzibar, Kilwa, etc. Several factories and their products from inland towns have been discussed by Dikshit (1949-52), and in chapter VI (pp. 74-75) I have described some extraordinary types. One of these harbours with bead-making factories was excavated by Sir Mortimer Wheeler (1946) and others near Pondichery in south India. The name of the site is Arikamedu and besides good numbers of trade-wind beads, many early Roman imports from the west (Arretine pottery, glass, coins, and wine-amphorae) have been found, all of the 1st century A.D.

Calcutta has a good collection of Indian stone and glass beads, but, as far as I can see, the collection at Allahabad Museum is better. The greater part of the material there comes from Kausambi near Allahabad.

A. MALAYA

Going farther east from Bengal, I have no records of beads coming from Burma or Thailand, but in Malaya we shall soon cross the tracks of emigrants from India, passing the isthmus of Kraa as early as the 5th century A.D. It was a short cut from a route that was already established some centuries earlier by Indian travellers going to colonize Sumatra, and later Java as well. There was always, however, the danger of the Atjeh pirates and this was one of the reasons for taking the overland route via Kraa. This seemed to be a shorter way to the banks of the Mekong river, which offered a safe passage to Ayuthia and other famous and rich towns in the 4th to the 7th centuries. On that overland route stone beads like cornelian and amethyst and quartz were abundant, according to Quaritsch Wales (1937), who travelled there and tells us that the common Indian trade-wind beads were scarce. More interesting is a famous old mart near what is now Kuala Selinsing, where on some spots the beach is strewn with trade-wind beads including large globular cornelians and square biconical cylinder beads, more than 25 mm. long, of cornelian as well (Beck, 1930).

Johore llama, Old Johore, is the next place of interest, and is also an ancient mart. Situated near the southern shore of the peninsula, it must have been a port of call from the beginning of our era, as it is mentioned in the Periplus (Schoff, 1912), and the beads (Gardner, 1937) seem to agree with such a dating. What will first strike us in the Gardner collection, now in the Raffles Museum in Singapore, are some twenty large beads of black glass, all ornamented with white, yellow or red lines or blue, black or white eyes. Everybody who studies beads will instantly think of Phoenician or Syrian beads around the beginning of our era. The next row of beads may all be multiple-wound beads, reminding us of examples of the 2nd to the 4th centuries A.D. in India. Amongst these there are a lot of black beads, again of larger size, up to 12 to 15 mm., zoned with a white line around the greatest diameter, so that they imitate onyx beads. Stone beads of cornelian, quartz, and red and green jasper in sizes up to 18 mm., are followed by many smaller beads, including some garnets. Another surprise are a number of faience beads, mostly small short double cylinder beads, half a dozen typical Egyptian melon beads, and a few long cylinder beads of the mummy-net type. Several amber beads, too, look like strangers in this company. Then follow the common Indian trade-wind beads and lastly a few dozen Indian-red, distinctly wound oval barrel beads of 12 by 6 mm. All these were picked up on the surface of what must have been a port of call for the last two thousand years.

Indian colonization did not stop at the Malayan peninsula. Travelling north from the Bandon Bight at the end of the Kraa overland route the famous Angkor towns could be reached, where, so far, only a few small Indian beads have been found; or, moving farther east, the interesting Oc-èo in the Mekong delta could be reached, where thousands of stone beads made from all kinds of minerals have been found and hundreds of trade-wind beads were collected by Louis Malleret of the French School of the Extreme Orient (Malleret, 1951).

B. INDONESIA

Turning now to the Indonesian archipelago we find widely spread over Sumatra and Java a large amount of Indian trade-wind beads in stone slab graves.

I am sure that when, in the near future, contacts are easier between Indonesia and Holland very interesting facts will be published. At

BEADS from Indonesian island of Flores, described by H. C. Beck (*Archaeologia*, 77 [1928]) as Romano-Egyptian, but all made in Amsterdam except cornelian beads in first row. In second row : three mulberry beads, one gilt glass bead and three chevron beads; in third, pentagon beads of clear, amber or brown glass; in fourth, glass oblates, clear, amber or blue.

present I can mention as particularly interesting only Rouffaer's « muti-sala » beads (fig. 74), the famous holy beads of Timor and Flores, that have been found in small quantities in Sumatra and Java too (Rouffaer, 1899).

These muti-sala are very small, wound ring-beads of 3 to 4 mm. diameter, varying in colour from brownish red to yellow. We shall meet them again on Flores, where they work their way up from the soil to lie on top of the grass which sprouts after the burning of the wild grass (alang). That is why the beads are very valuable, so that a small necklace buys a bride and one small bead a sheep or goat. Other strange beads found in connexion with the stone slab graves are what I call

« Chinese beads », as I know them from, e.g., the Chernuchi Museum in Paris (for good reproductions see Van Heekeren, 1958, pl. 13). They are globular or oval beads, often 25 mm. long, made of dark green glass, ornamented with many « eyes » consisting of a lighter green elongated spot surrounded by a yellow line. I know the same type of decoration from Persia, probably belonging to the first centuries of our era.

The eastern part of the archipelago brings us more beads which we have not yet met. On Bali I found typical Indian-red beads, but now not drawn but wound. They are heavy, and the chemical analysis shows more than 25 % of lead. The muti-sala, however, contained more than 35 % and beautiful wine-red transparent beads with many air-bubbles contained more than 50 % as PbO. Since Chinese and Japanese scholars tell me that their countries never exported glass beads for barter or trade, we must conclude that somewhere in south-east Asia there must have been factories making beads from lead glass for at least a thousand years. Nowadays Japan has a flourishing bead industry, and all the glass beads I know from their factories are very heavy lead glass.

No determined collecting of glass beads has taken place in Indonesia. Some people gathered a few necklaces, but after one or two generations they forgot where they came from and they are lost to science. It is high time that the beads in Djakarta Museum were studied. At the same time special care should be devoted to looking out for ancient beads kept as souvenirs by all people who have worked in this area.

A very interesting collection, for example, was assembled by a few Roman Catholic priests who spent a long time on the Indonesian island of Flores. Their collection was sent to me for identification and brought to Holland for the first time the sacred muti-sala beads from Flores that Rouffaer (1899) tried to describe. He mentions a number of references to these beads, beginning with Rumphius (1702). The greater part of this collection is now in a Mission Museum at Weert in Holland. A small number is in my own collection. The following beads proved to be of special interest :

1. Mulberry beads in clear, blue and amber coloured glass (Beck, 1928, p. 26 : Egypt, Roman period) (fig. 78).
2. Gold-leaf beads, having gold leaf between two layers of glass. (Roman according to Beck) (fig. 79).
3. Chevron or star beads (Beck, 1928, p. 65 : Egypt, Roman period) (fig. 80).
4. Amber pentagon beads (Beck's twisted square beads; Beck, 1928, p. 17 : Egypt, Roman period) (fig. 81).

5. A few dozen cornelian beads.
6. Several garnet beads and imitations in glass.
7. Indian-red and orange trade-wind beads.
8. Hundreds of the small sacred muti-sala beads.
9. Dozens of wine-red oval beads of lead glass (fig. 75).
10. Dozens of wine-red globular lead-glass beads, some squared by pinching (fig. 77).
11. Yellow, white and red small and large modern beads.
12. A dozen typical ornamented Venetian beads.

I have put n°s 1-4 first, because in Chapter XII (p. 110) we shall see that these four types were made in large quantities in Amsterdam in the 17th century by the merchants of the Dutch East India Company for barter with aborigines.

The others beads in this list which require special comment are those in groups 7, 8, 9 and 10. All these beads feel very heavy and they sink readily in Bromoform, which means that their specific gravity is over 3. The analyses show why. The first five beads on the list all show a large content of lead (PbO, lead oxide). All these beads are wound beads :

Beads from	1	2	3	4	5	6	7
	Flores Muti-Sala	Bali	Flores	Bali	Johore	Flores	Amsterdam
Colour	Orange brown opaque	Orange brown opaque	Wine-red transparent		Yellow Opaque	Amber transparent	Amber
Form	small ringlets	oblates 4 mm.	ellipsoids 8 mm.	ellipsoids 8 mm.	Oval 15 mm.	15 mm.	15 mm.
SiO_2	34,40	39,61	45,87	41,37	45,90	66,02	—
Fe_2O_3	2,49	1,79	0,15	0,109	0,12	0,148	—
TiO_2	0,30	0,31	0,025	0,0125	0,138	—	—
Al_2O_3	2,83	2,28	0,70	0,65	0,35	0,39	—
CaO	4,47	4,16	0,56	0,77	0,42	9,68	—
MgO	1,24	—	0,23	traces	0,45	0,43	—
Na_2O	1,46	0,88	1,10	traces	8,44	traces	0,44
K_2O	9,95	13,16	3,37	6,63	1,78	23,14	22,98
Cu_2O	4,50	1,60	—	traces	—	—	—
SnO_2	—	—	—	—	—	—	—
P_2O_5	0,056	0,192	—	—	—	—	—
MnO	0,115	—	0,0252	—	0,005	0,017	—
SO_3	—	—	—	—	—	0,15	—
Cr_2O_3	—	—	—	—	—	—	—
CuO	—	—	—	—	—	—	—
FeO	—	—	—	—	—	—	—
PbO	37,92	26,00	47,58	50,40	41,05	—	—
Au	—	present	present	—	—	—	—
Period	?	?	?	?	?	A.D. 1600	A.D. 1600

The last two analyses show no lead, but have an extraordinarily high content of potash (kalium oxide). They are products of a 17th-century Amsterdam factory that nearly always used potash instead of soda in making glass.

Now lead-glass beads are very rare in Europe and in Africa. In India you may meet a few. In Japan all new beads are rich in lead, but the directors of Japanese and Chinese museums say (p. 99) that their countries never exported glass beads for barter or commerce.

The finding of many lead glass beads in Indonesia might point to import from countries like Annam, Tongking, Laos, etc., perhaps even from the Philippines, or — might it be from eastern Europe, Russia, the Balkans or even Samarkand, where many of the artisans, taken by Timurlane from Syria and Palestine, must have restarted their handicraft in the new surroundings?

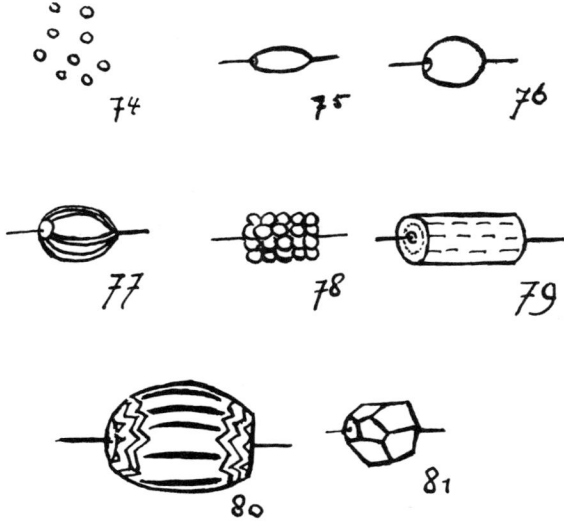

PLATE VI
Beads from the Indonesian island of Flores.

C. CHINA

Many beads from China came to Holland, mostly as necklaces with alternating wood, bone, ivory and porcelain beads. Jade beads could be found also, often beautifully cut, but I have never seen glass beads, except perhaps the strings of small glass beads that adorn many Chinese lanterns. These however are probably imported.

D. JAPAN

In the old days Japan had many beads, made of rough jade, specially of dark forms, called nephrite. Indian trade-wind beads came to the Ueno Museum in Tokyo, and glass imitations of tiger-claws, can be found in many kinds of stone and in glass too. Nowadays all kinds of wound beads are made, but they are all of very heavy lead glass. There are to-day more than 5000 small domestic bead factories in Japan and a dozen glass-works that make rods for drawn beads.

News of still greater interest will come some day from Japan. In the 8th century a wise man had a beautiful house (the Shosoin treasury) built, and collected in it all kinds of househould objects and paintings and statues and all kinds of objects of art, that might be interesting for future generations. He had the house sealed and locked and arranged that the seals should only be broken after a thousand years had gone by. When the Shosoin treasury was opened at the given time, not only objects were found, but also many documents, containing a full description of how to make glass beads, including the composition of the batch and the fuel that should be used. Unfortunately the knowledge of the ancient Japanese language has not yet developed so far, that this manuscript, and of course many others, can be translated. We know, however, that small green beads were made in the days of the ancient burial mounds, beads of low specific gravity, which indicates that lead-glass beads were not yet made in Japan in the 4th to 7th centuries A.D.

CHAPTER X

Beads from West Africa

In the vast developing young states of Ghana, Nigeria, Ivory Coast, etc., we find beads that are absolutely different from all those we found on the eastern coast. The Indian beads hardly reached the west coast, although there must already have been for many centuries a trade-route from Cairo as well as from Ethiopia through the Sahara to Lake Chad and farther on to the Niger, where, for example, cornelian beads are well known. But the great bulk of beads that many travellers describe and buy as indigenous (fig. 60) are the typical mosaic and some (fig. 61) millefiori beads, that have been imported there from Venice for at least two or three hundred years. They are 25 mm. long, round or square cylinder beads of a very special make. First a number of glass rods must be made by rolling (marvering) a thin rod of black or blue glass over a white glass plate, that sticks all around the rod. Then in the same way brown or blue or red or whatever colour is wanted is added, until a diameter of 5, 6 or 8 mm. is reached. A slice cut off such a rod shows concentric circles of different colours. If one or more of the rollings has been done not on a flat piece of marble or steel but on a sharply ribbed surface it produces a flower design. If the ribs on the marver are rounded, with deep ridges in between, they produce a star. If the work is begun, not with a thin rod, but with a bead or perforated bulb of glass, and blue and white, brown and white, and lastly blue again are added, always rolling on ribbed plates, the result is the famous chevron beads, which can be made in all sizes by pulling out the large cylinder formed thus to produce even the smallest chevron beads of 5 mm. diameter.

This method may also be used to make rods with all kinds of sections, even showing a human face. Small slices of such rods are cut and melted into a matrix of black or other cheap glass and so form the mosaic or millefiori beads. The oldest 25-mm.-long cylinder beads of this type in west Africa are generally milk-white or yellow, with only one coloured slice put in; later 6, 8 or 10 slices were affixed to one bead-matrix and heated and rolled until the mosaic bead was ready and the whole surface perfectly smooth.

All over west Africa there are also many African-made beads.

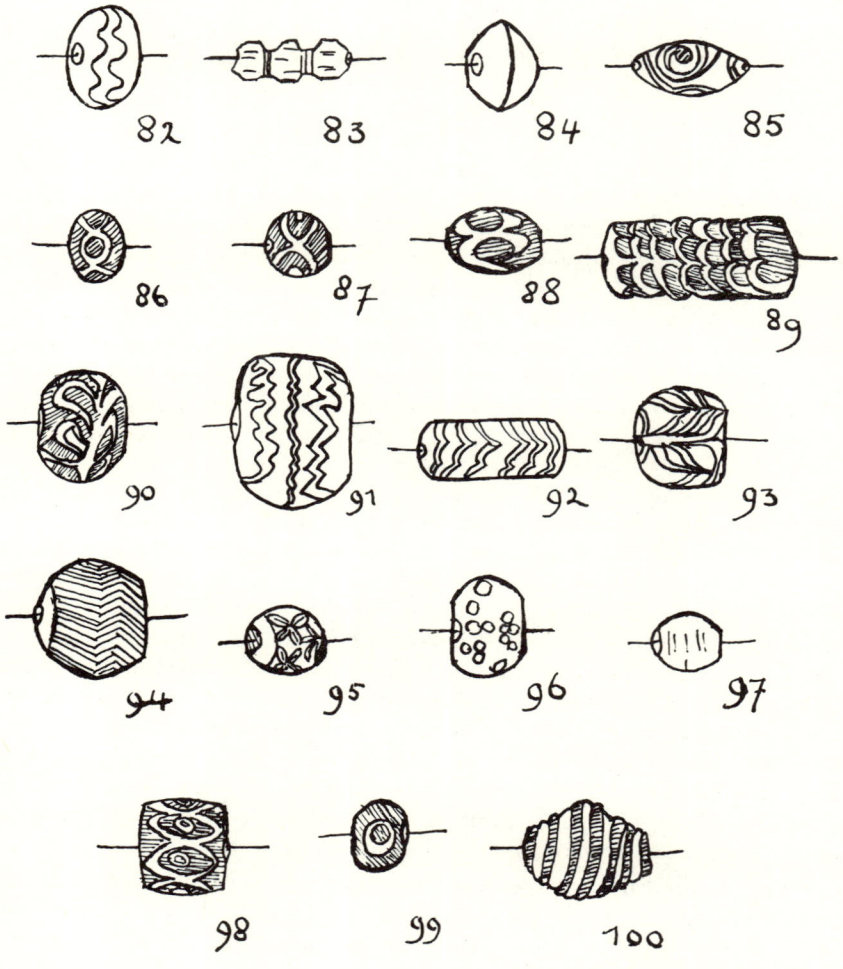

PLATE VII
Ancient beads from Europe.
Beads of Merovingian times A.D. 450-750.

CHAPTER XI

Ancient beads in Europe

Glass making started in Europe a long time after Mesopotamian and Egyptian glass spread over the Mediterranean countries. Glass and glass beads were imported over the lower mountain passes such as the Brenner and along the rivers, the Danube, the Rhône and the Rhine. From the north came amber pendants and beads of amber, the beautiful yellow to orange and brown fossil resin of pine trees, mostly collected around the Baltic. From the south along the rivers came Phœnician

    1   AMSTERDAM BEADS   2

1. Top and bottom rows, handmade wound beads, quite primitive. The rest are drawn beads and tubes.
2. First bead at left in top row is a pentagonal cylinder; the rest are drawn beads except first four beads in fourth row, which are pentagon beads, and bottom row.

(Photographs by the author)

105

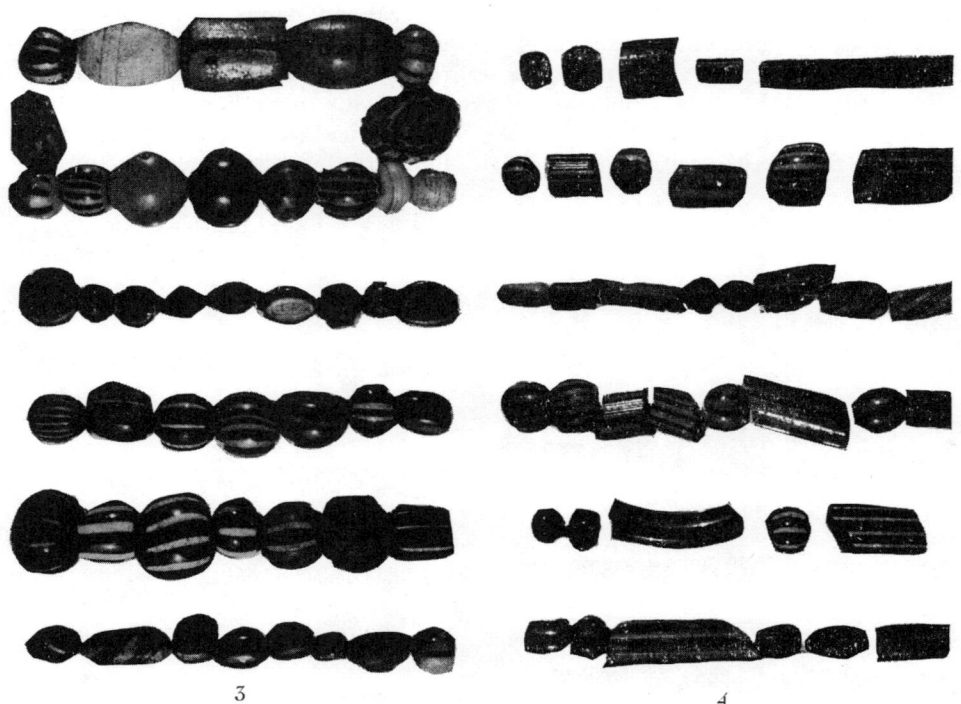

AMSTERDAM BEADS
3. Beads found in market gardens near Amsterdam. The three middle beads in each of the two upper rows are older, wound beads; the rest are drawn beads of Venetian style.
4. Some striped beads and tubes.

beads among which were the wide-spread eye-beads. But it looks as if the evil eye was losing its significance so that, if eyes are shown, they are cramped in by single or double wavy lines or reduced to simple spots. (Plate VII figs. 98, 99). Later an immense variety of types appears. Beads of large size, elongated barrels and square cylinders of 30 mm. were common; also quantities of beads of black Syrian glass (Aquileia).

Spread over the whole Roman Empire and later farther north and west, we find the melon bead in blue cobalt glass or bluish green faience. Merovingian beads from the cemeteries had followed the same import routes (see the publications of the Römisch-Germanische Kommission). They are highly ornamented (Plate VII). Others are of a great simplicity, opaque and in different colours : grey, yellow, blue or red. The whole of Europe shows the same picture.

Pipe and pipe bowls, of types known to have been made between 1610 and 1650, found in the same fields as the Amsterdam beads.

CHAPTER XII

Beads from 17th-century Amsterdam

In 1960, when I had just proved how all ancient beads found in East Africa had been imported from and made in India, I heard that strange beads had been found on arable land in 's Graveland, not quite five miles from my home. We collected a few hundred beads of different colours and sizes and I was rather astonished to see that there were amongst them some rather misshapen ones (fig. 109-111) and that there were also many small glass tubes (fig. 105, 106), about 25 mm. long and up to 6 mm. in diameter, such as are used to make drawn beads. It was clear that a bead factory must have worked in the neighbourhood and the refuse spread in one way or another over the land.

We have known for a long time that in the 17th century there were glass factories in Amsterdam, making bottles and beer- and wine-glasses and even « crystallyne mirrors ». A little search in the literature showed that Hudig (1923) had mentioned that a certain factory had the permission to make « *paternoster-werke* », which is the old Dutch word for rosary. Jan Heinrixszn Soop, who called himself in his petitions to the government « the Master of the Glass Furnace », had succeeded in smuggling out of Venice some well known master-glassmakers with all their utensils and put them in 1613 to work in the heart of Amsterdam, employing sixty Dutch families as well. That at once makes it clear why we find very coarse products (fig. 101-104), probably the first attempts at bead-making, amongst many much finer, more variegated types, as we shall soon see.

Glass ovens and remains of the glass-working were found again when digging out foundations on the famous Keizersgracht. The Dutch beads were soon made so well (fig. 113-120) that we should not have been able to distinguish them from the Venetian ones, had there not been a difference in the chemical composition. Venice nearly always used soda for glass-making and soda was a product of the Orient. Potash was an article won by burning peat and wood in our stoves and factories and bakers' ovens. Some Dutch beads contain more than 20 % of potash, designated as K_2O. In this way I showed that the beautiful amber-coloured beads from Bali and Flores were from good old Dutch stock (see analyses on p. 100).

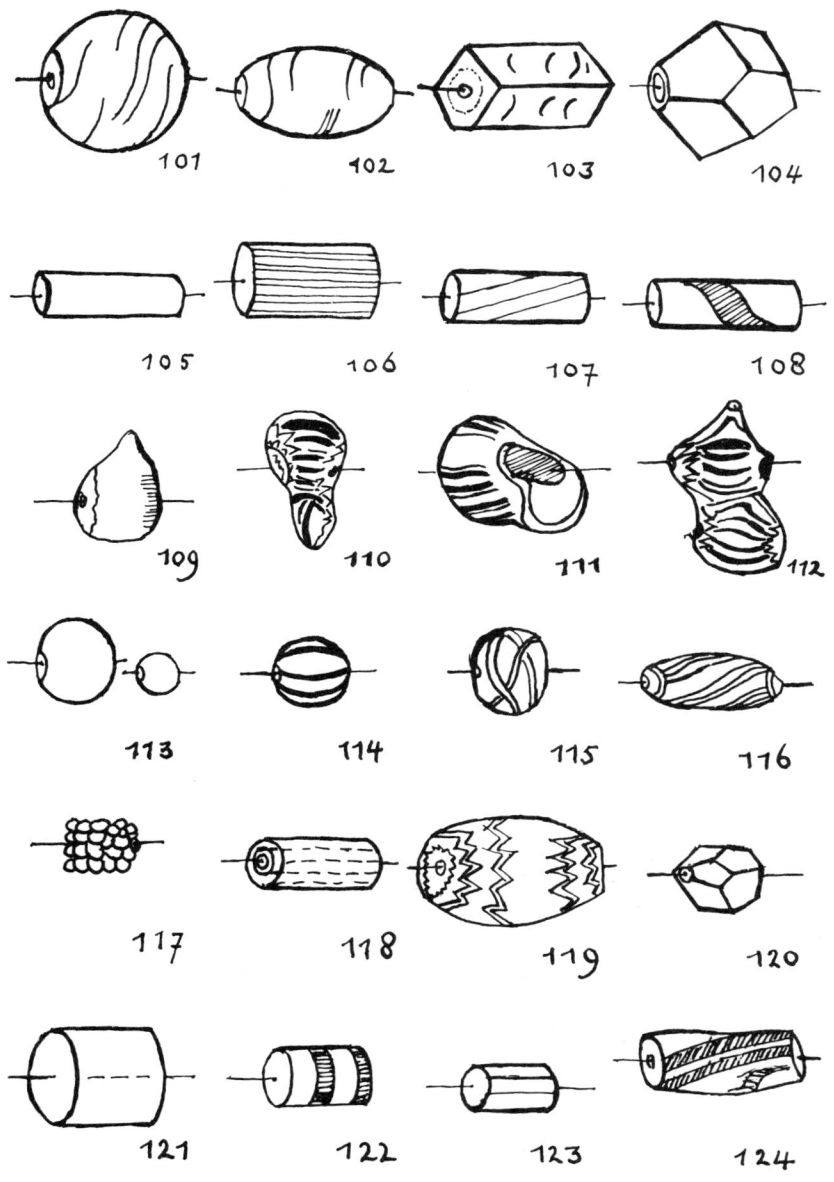

PLATE VIII
Beads from the Amsterdam factory, fig. 101-120 in the 17th Century.
Beads made by African natives, fig. 121-124.

Continuing my search for more material, I met a greengrocer whose family had always worked the soil at the canals outside Amsterdam. In caring for his produce he had collected another few hundred beads and still more tubes of nicely-coloured striped glass, exactly such as I had found in 's Graveland — the refuse of a large glass-factory. But he and I had collected many other things also. There were a large number of bowls of broken tobacco-pipes, often of very small dimensions and bearing marks or numbers which showed that they had been made before 1650. There were also sherds of broken German stoneware, mostly blue-on-grey, ornamented with coats of arms, and bearing dates, 1632, 1640, 1644, and so on, as well as broken Chinese, and Japanese Imari, porcelain. There were baked-clay marbles, too, and chemists' weights of lead, and, indeed, everything you might expect to find in the refuse of a rich 17th-century town.

People in Venice just as well as those in Amsterdam threw all their rubbish into the canals, and these had to be cleaned from time to time, to let the ships come through. All this rubbish and mud was looked upon as manure. Now in the 17th century Amsterdam wanted sand to build up the roads along the canals, and such sand could be obtained on the flats at Bussum and Hilversum where, when the sand had been taken away, the élite of those days, Tromp and friends of Hooft, Vondel and Rembrandt, built summer houses. The ships, which came for more sand, brought the manure to fertilize the new gardens. With the manure came the mud from the canals and the refuse of the town. These old gardens now form the splendid 350-year-old beech woods providing large recreational centres for the population of Amsterdam.

In studying these Amsterdam beads, I suddenly recognized four of them which had been in each other's company before, namely the mulberry beads (fig. 117), the gold-leaf (fig. 118), the chevron (fig. 119) and the pentagon beads. (fig. 120) They came then (p. 99) from Flores and were assigned by Beck to Romano-Egyptian times. Now we understand that they were made in Amsterdam, which is a much more probable proposition.

Many other Dutch beads were sent to me from the Antilles, where, for example, on St Eustatius island large blue beads are still washed on to the shore where before 1750 the large warehouses of the Dutch West India Company had stood.

Quite a series of Dutch beads were, without his recognizing their origin, illustrated by Peter Pratt (1961) in his booklet about the beads of the Fort Stanwix Museum in Rome, N.Y. They are depicted also by

Orchard (1929). I wonder when the Hudson Bay Company will tell us what kind of beads their « adventurers » brought to the Canadian Indians ?

In fig. 101-104 you will find reproductions of what I have already called very coarse products. This group consists mostly of very large beads that often look worn or weathered. The greater part are blue, seldom clear, and mostly half opaque. You may find them, too, in black, white, brown or a beautifully-clear amber colour, those in this last colour generally being smaller specimens up to 15 mm., while the larger ones are up to 25 mm. long and 18 to 20 mm. in diameter. They are rarely globular; half of them are oval or ellipsoid, quite a few are pentagonal and, of the rest, many are pentagonal cylinders. All are drawn beads, as is easily visible from spiral lines on the weathered specimens. The two last-mentioned forms have been pincered to make them angular. They are primitive beads, made of bad glass, often full of streaks, because the glass was made at too low a temperature. But they found their way all over the world.

The second group, probably made after the Venetian workers had joined the Amsterdam factory, looks much nicer, more attractive in colour, more shiny and technically of a much better finish. They are seldom weathered, have clear colours like cobalt blue and chrome-yellow and specially what in English is called Indian-red and is something between terracotta and brick-red, but often showing a beautiful polish. The colour in these beads is due to copper oxide. There are quite a few black beads too, often ornamented with two interweaving wavy lines or with longitudinal stripes. The former are wound, the latter drawn.

It is very interesting that among the Amsterdam beads, in Amsterdam as well as in west and east Africa, are found many very beautiful chevron or star beads (fig. 15, 119), generally composed of six different layers of coloured and white glass.

I have already said (p. 99) that Amsterdam beads found on Flores and Bali in Indonesia were first believed to be of Roman origin. There is another example of misinterpreted beads. Hercules Read (1905) described and illustrated a necklace from west Africa consisting of flat, circular shell beads and a number of amber pentagon beads and blue mulberry beads. To me they are as plainly Amsterdam beads as could be, though Read, according to the knowledge of his time, considered them as being left there by the Carthaginian Hanno who led an expedition to west Africa in the 5th century B.C. (fig. 117 and 120).

It will be very interesting to learn more about these Dutch beads, for they can show us the important trade-routes of the 17th and 18th centuries. As mentioned already, they are found in Canada, America, the Antilles, east and west Africa and Indonesia — quite a large portion of the then-known world. They occur in Europe as well. I have found them in Holland itself, at Amsterdam, Hoorn, Velzerend and Heemstede, and at the bottom of the large Haarlem Lake, when it was turned into land. Curiously enough a good number come from the island of Ameland, one of the Frisian islands. However, we know that from those islands many young men went to the whale fisheries and into the merchant marine. Many of the old commanders returned to their ancestral homes after their adventures on the seven seas and built there what are still known as the « *Commandeurshuisjes* ». No wonder that they brought home some of the trinkets which they used in bartering with natives all over the world, and these may now be seen in the Frisian Museum in Leeuwarden.

There is still another strange thing about the simple, coarse beads of the Amsterdam factory. In old Dutch villages such as Broek op Langendijk, just north of Amsterdam, we still find « *kralentuintjes* » or in English « bead gardens ». In some very old small gardens there are small, round flower-beds, mostly set round a pedestal that carries a sundial or the figure of a trumpeting angel. In the old days, there were no flowers in the beds, but they were, instead, « planted » with sections of large beads, coloured blue, white, milky blue and brown. Often the beads were laid with much care in coarse sand, so that the pattern could easily be changed.

CHAPTER XIII

Modern beads

A. VENICE

It is impossible to give a definition or description of the Venetian beads, because they exist in all imaginable forms and colours and if there is a type not made to-day, it may well be made to-morrow. New products leave the factory every year. The glass is made from its constituents in a large factory in Murano, a small island, reached within a quarter of an hour by boat from Venice itself. Glass-making was banished there because of the danger of fire in the town, that formerly had only wooden houses. Two products are made now, namely rods and tubes of glass, that are necessary for making wound and drawn glass beads, as described above (part I, fig. 1, 2). The work and the factory are described by Pasquato and Morazzoni (1953) and Gasparetto (1958). It seems most probable that in the 9th century, when St. Mark's was built, many mosaic-workers came from Byzantium and began glass-making according to Byzantine methods. Later, when Timurlane had taken most of the artisans out of Syria to Samarkand, perhaps Syrians also came to Venice and added their knowledge and efforts, to give Venice in the 13th century and for sometime afterwards what was practically a monopoly in glass- and bead-making in the western world. It is a great pity that we do not know what kinds and types of beads were produced. This secrecy continues till 1704, when a sample-book was issued, one specimen of which has found a place in the British Museum.

There are still things to be found out by careful study. When, for instance, were black beads first blackened by permanganate, whereas formerly iron was used ? It must have been around 1700. When was aventurine, the goldstone with its myriads of shining small copper crystals, first used, specially to replace gold foil in the ornamenting of beads « à la lampa » ? About 1850 ? When was selenium first used for producing bright red transparent beads, instead of the beautiful wine-colour, achieved with gold ? About 1930 ? When these questions are answered, it will be easier to date several finds belonging to the last few centuries.

B. GABLONZ or JABLONEC (CZECHOSLOVAKIA)

It seems that around the 15th century Venice exported glass tubes to Bohemia, where beads were made from them and then sold again by Venetian merchants. Soon after that the Bohemians began to make their own glass, making beads mostly for rosaries, and it was only in the beginning of the 19th century that they joined Venice in the world trade for bartering material. Nowadays they make a speciality of costume jewelry.

Since the beginning of this century they have changed the composition of their glass beads by adding a proportion of clay, or better felspar, to the batch, so that their product ought to be called porcelain beads. These beads are no longer drawn or wound, but are formed in a press, such as is used for making pastilles, and then baked. Although the beads are opaque, this process gives them an appealing lustre that distinguishes them from glass beads. Pressed beads can also often be distinguished from glass beads because of the equatorial band, sometimes hardly visible, which they possess.

In general the glass beads of Gablonz are not distinguishable from the products of Venice. They are perhaps a bit more regular and are often striped and mostly drawn. Chemical analysis might give clues. This is however not important. For us the great question is whether beads are modern European or not.

In the last decade many plastic beads have been made, which have the advantage of being so much lighter than glass.

C. KAUFBUEREN or NEU-GABLONZ (GERMANY)

Matters became still more complicated when many glass-workers, who did not like the iron curtain, emigrated and founded a new factory in Bavaria, south-east of Munich. Their products do not differ very much from what they made before, but you never can tell what they will make in the future.

D. BRIARE (BAPTEROSSES ET Cie), FRANCE

Unless you frequent the Congo or other central-African states, you will know these beads only from the Museum at Tervuren near

Brussels. They are mostly very typical cylinder beads, as straight as a military drum, called rocaille beads (fig. 68) in the trade. They are from 5 to 10 mm. in length and diameter. Globular and oval beads are fabricated as well, and, again, felspar is a real constituent of the mass, taking the place of some of the quartz. These beads may be found on very old wood-carvings in museums, but the factory at Briare only began working in 1840.

E. HEBRON

Although we think that Hebron had a glass factory hundreds of years before Christ, nowadays they make only very simple and rough beads. These are mostly eye-beads of 12 mm. diameter, blue, with a yellow eye and blue pupil. But there are also somewhat smaller eye-pendants in the same colour, and beads for necklaces of nearly square blocks of wound glass, about 18 mm. long with a huge perforation, in blue, Indian-red, yellow and green, often three colours in one bead. Their glass is now transparent, but a hundred years ago it was opaque, dark green and yellow only.

There are many small glass works all over the near east but, as far as I know, this is the only one making beads.

CHAPTER XIV

Aboriginal modern beads

A. AFRICA

The first kind to mention here are the ostrich-egg shell beads which I have seen made in south and central Africa several times, and that are found in exactly the same nicely rounded form in Sumerian Mesopotamia. The Kalahari Bushmen and several Bantu tribes still make them, sometimes for special occasions like initiation festivals. Imitations are often made from Achatina snail shells, this being a large land snail and therefore much thinner and not so strong, easily breakable and easily renewed, but never so nicely rounded and polished as the real ostrich-egg shell beads. Larger round discs are often made from Conus shells or even from ivory or bone. Larger beads still as, e.g., the Chimanda, a 100 mm. long cigar-shaped bead, much used in Kenya and the Congo, could only be made from the Giant clam, *Tridacna sp.*, the shell that is often seen as a baptismal font. In Kilwa, too, many large beads are made from this shell and sometimes from limestone also. In west Africa pretty beads are made from a rather clear jasper and from native bauxite (aluminium ore).

A few hundred years ago some Bantu in the northern Transvaal at Mapungubwe (Fouché, 1957) began making beads that were more to their liking, by melting together in a clay mould quantities of small, pulverized light green beads, so making the so-called garden-roller beads (fig. 119). The other beads at Mapungubwe are the common Indian trade-wind beads.

It may be a hundred years ago, too, that aborigines in what are now the Ivory Coast, Ghana and Nigeria began making beads from pulverized medicine-bottles. Two methods of bead-making have been published in *Man*. Wild (1937) tells how the natives make cylindrical holes 6-12 mm deep in a block of clay. They put part of the rib of a tapioca leaf in the centre of each hole and then fill the holes up with pulverized glass, preferably first some blue powder, then white and blue again *ad libitum* and after that fire the block of clay in a wood fire. The glass melts and sinters to a bead (fig. 122), the rib burns and leaves the perforation and the baked clay releases the beads easily. The result looks like fig. 122. Exactly the same method was perhaps used in Deir el Bahari about 1500 B.C.

Two years later Sinclair (1939) writes about natives first making small boat-like moulds of coarse, red baked clay. Then small, narrow lines of highly-coloured glass dust are laid lengthwise in the bottom of the mould. After that yellow or white glass powder is poured in till it rises above the sides of the mould. Then more lines of glass dust are laid on top and after firing a nice striped bead (fig. 123, 124) results, provided that a tiny straw or leaf-rib is placed on the half-filled mould so that it will burn and leave a perforation. Figs. 123, 124 show the beads, which are often bought by air-travellers passing through Kano or Leopoldville.

Nowadays somewhere in Ghana and in Bida in Nigeria more intricate glass beads are made, sometimes with spirals or twisted lines. We should take note of how these native artisans works as they will soon learn new techniques and forget their primitive ways, that are so interesting.

The small black beads, coloured by iron oxide, which are often found will burn and leave a perforation. Figs. 123, 124 show the beads, which as we find them in great numbers in Mapungubwe.

Those who buy strings of beads and necklaces in west Africa consisting of mosaic and millefiori beads about 25 mm. long should note that these were imported from Venice in shiploads in the last hundred years, though they are sold as ancient. They can be bought much more cheaply in Amsterdam, London or Venice.

B. NORTH AMERICA

The North-American Indians nowadays use huge quantities of small glass beads, so called seed-beads, to adorn their buckskin finery on social occasions such as, for instance, the Indian Days in Banff, Canada. Some tribes keep to geometric patterns in sewing the gaily-coloured beads on their dresses, while others prefer floral designs, that may be very elaborate and pretty. Thirty years ago I still saw quite a few shoulder-capes, worn by elderly women, which were adorned with pieces of long black and white porcupine quills, dyed in many colours and stitched on as if they were long glass cylinder beads, being just as shiny but more interesting. But what I could not find were wampum beads.

Captain Henry Hudson, who had already acquired tobacco and wheat from the Indians for a few knives and glass beads, must have been quite astonished when, on his second landing, he was presented by the Indians with a necklace of beads. If he had been a 20th-century traveller, he would have remembered arriving at Fiji and being hung all over with flower garlands as a sign of welcome. He could not know that the ornament he was given was known over the whole continent as a token of recognition from chief to chief, as a sign of friendship and honour. These necklaces and strings and belts had a definite role in trade and barter and had a fixed value as currency.

Wampum beads were cylinder beads of about 12 mm. long, made from a large clam shell, that was white when young, but soon got blue colouring, changing later to beautiful dark violet. The very hard shell had to be broken into squarish pieces, ground and polished to cylinders and then the most difficult work began – making the perforation. In pre-European days this had to be done with the aid of stone or quartz splinters, making conical holes from both sides which met in the middle. The beads were sewn on buckskin strips in special groups and sequences, that might be read by an insider, telling about historical events, like battles, land-purchase, and so on. All over Canada most articles were priced not only in beaver-skins, but also in strings of wampum beads. Several price lists are known (see, e.g., Orchard, 1929).

English Canadians soon began making wampum beads by the thousand with the aid of steel borers and other machinery, making a much narrower and straight perforation. But in the beginning of the 20th century wampum still held a certain value.

With the Europeans, glass beads of many different types came to America and Canada. Orchard (1929, p. 88) illustrates several of them, not knowing that all those beads and many others were imports from the Amsterdam factory. Pratt (1961), too, in publishing his marvellous colour pictures of beads found in Indian graves, did not know that he was advertising Dutch-made beads. I have since, however, corresponded with him and have published the information in *Archaeology* (van der Sleen, 1963). I am still trying to find out when and where the Hudson Bay Company imported these beads.

Both on the Atlantic and the Pacific coasts Indians used necklaces of *Dentalium* shells, the Elephant-tooth shell, that was worn in prehistoric Jericho seven thousand years ago.

On the west coast, also, buttons and disc beads made from Abalone (*Haliotis*) shells form part of the treasures of the Totem Indians. I saw them wearing them at the royal visit in Vancouver in 1939.

Several Americans have studied beads from Indian graves and one, Arthur Woodward (1959, 1960, 1965) has published a series of articles on their findings. Another well known investigator is Roderick Sprague.

Unfortunately most descriptions and even many drawings and photographs are too bad to allow me to identify the beads or to try to make out their date and origin. It will require much correspondence before I get the answer to all these questions.

C. SOUTH AMERICA

Gold beads will be found in many places in Central and South America. I know gilded clay beads from Ecuador, pottery beads or small spindle-whorls, with pelican reliefs from Peru, and many small turquoise and bone beads from Chile near Chuquicamata and the Anaconda mines. As far as I know there is very little literature about beads from these regions.

Bibliography

ALICU, M., 1963. « Bido glass workers », *Teacher*, vol. 7.
ARBMAN, H., 1939-41. *Die Gräber von Birka* (Stockholm).
ARKELL, A.J., 1936. « Cambay and the bead trade », *Antiquity*, vol. X.
ARMSTRONG, E.C.R., 1921. « Two Irish finds of glass beads of the Viking period », *Man*, vol. 21, n⁰ 40.
BECK, H.C., 1928. « Classification and nomenclature of beads and pendants », *Archaeologia*, vol. 77, pp. 1-76.
BECK, H.C., 1930. « Notes on sundry Asiatic beads », *Man*, n⁰ 134.
BECK, H.C., 1931. « Rhodesian beads », in G. CATON THOMPSON, *Zimbabwe Culture*.
BECK, H.C., 1941. « Beads from Taxila », *Mem. Archaeol. Surv. of India*, vol. 65, p. 1.
BECK, H.C., and SELIGMAN, C.G., 1932. « Chinese beads of foreign type », *Proc. First International Congr. of Prehistory, London, 1932* (Oxford).
BECK, H.C., 1934. « Glass before 1500 B.C. », *Ancient Egypt and the East*, 1934, pp. 7-21.
BELENITSKI, A.M., 1958. « Résultats de fouilles de la ville ancienne de Pendikent », *Sovjet Archaeology*, n⁰ 4.
BEZBORODOV, M.A., 1956. *Glassmaking in Ancient Russia* (Minsk).
BEZBORODOV, M.A., 1965. « Early stages of glassmaking in the U.S.S.R. », *Slavia antiqua*, vol. XII, pp. 127-142.
BOBROVA, O.S., 1949. « The beads of Afrasiab (Samarkand) », *Bull. Inst. Hist. Kratkie* n⁰ 30.
BÖHNER, Kurt, 1958. *Die Fränkischen Altertümer des Trierer Landes* (Berlin).
BOSTRAETEN, H.C., 1964. «Een Merovingische begraafplaats te Luthommel», *Taxandria*, blz. 9.
BOULANGER, J., 1909. *Le Cimetière franco-mérovingien et carolingien de Marché-le-pot* (Paris), pls. xi-xxii.
BROWN, G. Baldwin, 1915. *The Arts in Early England*, vol. IV (London).
BRUNTON, G., 1927. *Qau and Badari* (Brit. School of Archaeol. in Egypt, London).
BURTON, R.F., 1872. *Zanzibar* (London).
BUSHNELL, D.J., 1906. « Origin of wampum », *J. Royal Anthrop. Inst.*, vol. 36.
CALEY, E.R., 1962. *Analyses of Ancient Glasses* (Corning Museum of Glass, Monographs, I).
CALVI, M.C., *Roman Glass at Aquileia* (forthcoming).
CATON THOMPSON, G., 1931. *The Zimbabwe Culture* (Oxford), pp. 242, et al.
CHMIELOVSKA, A., 1960. « Les parures en verre du Xᵉ siècle de Gdansk », *Gdansk Wczesnos redniowieczny*, III, p. 105.
CHROPOVSKI, B., 1965. « Das Slavische Gräberfeld in Nitra am Lupka », *Slovenska Archeologia*, X. 1 (Bratislava).
CLARK, J.G.D., 1952. *Prehistoric Europe* (London).
COCHET (Abbé), 1859. *La tombe de Childéric Iᵉʳ* (Paris).
CSALLANY, D., 1961. « Altertumsk. Denkm. der Gepiden », *Hung. Akad. der Wiss.*
DANIEL, F., 1937. « Beadworkers of Iloring, Nigeria », *Man*, 1937, n⁰ 2.
DANNHEIMER, H., 1962. *Germanische Funde der späten Kaiserzeit* (Röm. Germ. Komm.).
DAPPER, O., 1676. *Nauwkeurighe beschrijvinghe der Afrikaanse gewesten* (Amsterdam).
DAVIDSON, G.R., 1952. *Corinth. XII. The Minor Objects* (Princeton).
DÉCHELETTE, J., 1924. *Manuel d'Archéologie Préhistorique* (Paris).
DEKOVNA, M., 1962. « Verre de provenance étrangère », *Slavia antiqua*, IX.
DEOPIK, V.B., 1959. « Classif. of the 4th-5th cent. beads of the north. Caucasus », *Sovjet Archaeology*, n⁰ 3.

DIACONU, G., 1965. « Tirgsor, Necropoli di sec. III-IV », *Bibl. de Arch*. vol. VIII, (Bucarest).
DIKSHIT, M.G., 1949. *Etched Beads in India* (Deccan Coll. Mon. Series, Poona).
DIKSHIT, M.G., 1952. « Beads from Ahichchhatra », *Ancient India*, vol. 8.
DIKSHIT, M.G., 1952. *Some Beads from Kundapur* (Hyderabad Archaeol. Series, vol. 16).
DIKSHIT, M.G., 1955. *Tripuri* (Univ. of Saugar), pp. 85-95.
DU TOIT, A.P., 1964. « Glass beads as a medium of dating archaeological sites », *South African Journal of Sciences*, pp. 98-99.
EISEN, G., 1916. « Eye-beads from the earliest time to the present », *Amer. Journ. of Archaeology*, 2 series, n° 20.
FIEDLER, Resi, 1963. « Die vor- und frühgeschichtl. Funde in Dettingen Kirchheim unter Tek», *Veröffentl. der Staatl. Anstalt f. Denkmalpflege*, Heft 7 (Stuttgart).
FINGERLIN, G., 1962. « Das Alemannische Gräberfeld von Binningen im Hegau, Landkreis Konstanz », *Badische Fundberichte*, 22ste Jahrgang.
FINGERLIN, G., 1964. « Grab einer adligen Frau aus Güttingen, Landkreis Konstanz », *Badische Fundberichte*, Heft 4.
FINGERLIN, G., *Grabfunde aus Singen*. Forthcoming.
FOUCHÉ, L., 1957. *Mapungubwe* (Cambridge), pp. 26, 103-113.
FOURNEAU, J., 1952. « Sur les perles anciennes de Zanaga », *Bull. de l'IFAN*, p. 216.
FRANKEN, M., 1944. *Die Alemannen zwischen Iller und Lech* (Röm.-Germ. Kommission).
FREMERSDORF, F., 1955. *Der Fränkische Reihengräberfeld Köln-Müngersdorf* (Germ. Denkmäler der Völkerwand. Zeit, Berlin, vol. VI).
GARDNER, G.S., 1937. « Ancient beads from the Johore River », *J. Roy. Asiat. Soc.* (London).
GASPARETTO, A., 1958. *Sulla storia delle conterie Veneziane* (Venice).
GLAZEMA, P. and YPEY, J., 1956. *Merovingische Ambachtkunst* (Baarn, Holland).
GREGORY, H.A. and WEBB, Clarence H., 1965. « European trade beads from six sites in Natchitoches parish, Louisiana », *Florida Anthropologist*, vol. XVIII, n° 3, part 2, pp. 15-44, ill.
HAEVERNICK, Th. E., 1961. « Chevron beads ». *Jahrb. Röm.-Germ. Zentral Mus. Mainz*, vol. 8.
HARDEN, D.B., 1933. « Ancient glass », *Antiquity*, vol. VII.
HARDEN, D.B., 1962. *Annales du 2e Congrès des Journées Internationales du Verre à Leyde, Hollande*, p. 86.
HEEKEREN, H.R. van, 1958. « The bronze-iron age in Indonesia », *Verhandl. Inst. Land, Taal en Volkenkunde*, deel 22.
HEJDOVA, Dagmar, 1965-1966. « Bibliographie des plus importantes trouvailles archéologiques de verre en Tchécoslovaquie », *Bulletin des Journées Internationales du Verre*, n° 4, pp. 100-106, n°s 9-12, 13-17, 18-29, 30-38, 45-49, 59-93, 97-99.
HELL, M. L., « Färbige Glasperlen aus Ober Oesterreich », *Archeol. Austr.*, vol. 14.
HENSEL, W., 1961. *Starodawna Kruszwicka* (Wroclaw).
HETTES, K., 1960. *Venezianer Glas* (Prague).
HIRTH, Fr., and ROCKHILL, W.W., 1911. *Chau Yu Kua. Chinese and Arab trade in the 12th and 13th Centuries*.
HONEY, W.B., 1946. *Victoria and Albert Museum. Glass. A Handbook for the Study of Glass Vessels of all Periods and Countries and a Guide to the Museum Collection* (London).
HOOP, J. van der, 1932. *Megalithic Remains in South Sumatra* (Zutphen).
HOURANI, G.F., 1951. *Arab Seafaring* (Princeton).
HRUBY, V., 1955. *Staré Mesto, velkomoravské pohrebiste* « *Na Valach* » (Praha).
HUDIG, F.W., 1923. *Das Glas* (Vienna).
HUNTINGFORD, G.W.B., 1950. *East African Background* (London).
JASKANIS, J., 1956. « Sklane paciorski, etc. Les perles en verre », *Wiadomosci Archeologiozne*, vol. 23, n° 2.

KIRKMAN, J.S., 1954. *The Arab City of Gedi* (Oxford).
KISA, A., 1908. *Das Glas im Altertume* (Leipzig).
KNOWLES, W.J., 1881. « Ancient Irish beads », *J. Roy. Hist. and Archaeol. Ass. of Ireland*, vol. 25.
KRAEMER, W., 1964. « Das keltische Gräberfeld von Nehringen », *Veröff. Staatl. Anst. f. Denkmalpflege*, Heft 8 (Stuttgart).
KRIEGER, K., 1943. « Studien über Afrikanische Kunstperlen », *Baseler Archiv*.
KRUMPHANSLOVA, Z., 1965. *Glasperlen der Burgwallzeit* (Ceskosl. Akad., Prague).
LAIDLER, P.W., 1934, 1935, 1937. *Beads in Africa, South of the Zambesi* (Rhodesia Scientific Association, Salisbury).
LAL, B.B., 1953. « Examination of some ancient Indian glass specimens », *Ancient India*, vol. 8.
LAMB, A., 1966. « A note on glass beads from the Malay peninsula », *Journal of Glass Studies*, vol. VIII, pp. 80-94.
LAMM, C.J., 1941. *Oriental Glass of Medieval Date* (Stockholm).
LETHBRIDGE, T.C., 1936. *Report of the excavation of a cemetery of the Christian-Anglo-Saxon Period* (Cambridge Antiquarian Society, Cambridge).
LOESCHCKE, S., 1925. *Trierer Heimatbuch* (Festschrift).
LORENTZ, S., 1963. « Collections de verre de Pologne », *Bulletin des Journées Internationales du Verre*, n° 2.
LOWE, C. van Riet, 1937. « Beads of the water », *Bantu Studies*, vol. XI.
LWOWA, Z.A., 1958. « Classification of glass beads of Premongolian Russia », *Bulletin State Hermitage Museum, Leningrad*, n° 4.
LWOWA, Z.A., 1959. « Les bracelets et perles en verre de Sarkele-Belaja-Vega », *Matériaux et Recherches* (Leningrad), n° 75.
LWOWA, Z.A., 1961. *Les bijoux de verre de l'Europe Orientale du 8e jusqu'au 12e siècle* (Edition de l'Hermitage).
MALLERET, L., 1951. « Oc-Eo », *Bull. de l'Ecole Française en Extr. Orient*, vol. XLV.
MARCHESETTI, C., 1893. *Scavi della Necropoli di S. Lucia* (Trieste).
MARSHALL, Sir John, 1931. *Mohenjo-Daro and the Indus Civilization* (London).
MARSHALL, Sir John, 1952. *Taxila*, II (Cambridge).
MAUNY, R., 1949. « Perles de cornaline, quartz et verre des tumuli du Bas Sénégal », *Notes Africaines*, t. XLIII.
MILLOT, J., 1952. « Considérations sur le commerce dans l'Océan Indien au Moyen Age », *Mém. de l'Inst. Scient. de Madagascar*, série C.I.
MIYOSHI. *Beads of Japan, Philipp. Islands and South Sea* (Tokyo).
NERI, A., 1612. *L'Arte Vetraria in Libri Sette* (Florence).
NIEUWENHUIS, A.W., 1904. « Kunstperlen und ihre culturelle Bedeutung », *Intern. Archiv. für Ethnologie*, vol. XVI.
ORCHARD, W.C., 1929. *Beads and Beadwork of the American Indians* (New York).
PASQUATO, M., and MORAZZONI, G., 1953. *Le Conterie Veneziane* (Venice), pp. 1-83.
PEARCE, F.B., 1920. *Zanzibar* (London).
PENDLEBURY, J.D.S., 1951. *The City of Akhenaton* (London).
PETRIE, W.M.F., 1902. *Abydos* (London).
PETRIE, W.M.F., 1914. *Amulets* (London).
PIGGOTT, S., 1949. *British Prehistory*.
PRATT, P.P., 1961. *Oneida-Iroquois Glass Trade Beads* (Rome, New York).
QUIGGIN, A.H., 1949. *Trade Routes, Trade and Currency in East Africa* (Occasional papers of the Rhodes-Livingstone Museum).
READ, C. Hercules, 1905. « A necklace of glass beads from West Africa », *Man*, vol. V, n° 1.

REINECKE, P., 1902-1911. *Die Altertümer unserer heidnischen Vorzeit*, vol. V.
RENOU, L. and FILIOZAT, J., 1947-1953. *L'Inde classique* (Paris).
RICHTER, G.M.A., 1940. *Handbook of the Etruscan Collection in the Metr. Mus.*, New York.
RIVETT-CARNAC, J.H., 1900. « Ancient Indian beads », *Journ. of Indian Art and Industry*, vol. IX.
ROUFFAER, G.P., 1899. « Waar kwamen de Muti-sala van Timor vandaan ? », *Bijdr. voor Land-Taal en Volkenkunde van Ned. Indie*, reeks 6, deel 6.
RUMPHIUS, G.E., 1702. *Het Amboinse kruidboek* (Amsterdam).
SALIN, E., 1939. *Le haut Moyen Age en Lorraine* (Paris).
SANDE, G.A.J. VAN DER, 1907. *Nova Guinea*, III (Leiden).
SANKALIA, H.D., and DIKSHIT, M.G., 1952. *Excavations at Brahmapuri (Kolhapur)* (Deccan Coll. Monogr. Series, vol. V).
SCAPOVA, J.L., 1962. « O proishozednii nekotoryh tipov drevnerusskih bus », *Sovetskaja Archeologija*, n° 2, pp. 81-96.
SCHMIDT, B., 1961. *Die späte Völkerwanderungszeit in Mittel-Deutschland* (Veröff. des Landesmus. für Vorgeschichte in Halle).
SCHOFF, W.H., 1912. *The Periplus of the Erythraean Sea* (New York).
SCHOFIELD, W.F., 1938. « Prehistoric beads of the Transvaal and Natal », *Transact. Roy. Soc. S. Africa*, vol. XXIV.
SCHOFIELD, W.F., 1943. « A study of the old trade beads of Nyassaland », *Transact. Roy. Soc. S. Africa*, vol. XXX.
SCHÜLE, W., 1965. « Die Reihengräber von Walsheim », *Bericht Staatl. Denkmalpflege in Saarland* (Beitr. Archeologie, Saarbrücken).
SELIGMAN, C.G., and BECK, H.C., 1938. *Far Eastern Glass : Some Western Origins* (Bull. Mus. Far Eastern Antiquities, Stockholm, vol. X).
SHCHAPOVA, I.U., 1956. « Glass beads in ancient Novgorod », *Research in Archaeology, U.S.S.R.*, n° 55.
SHCHAPOVA, I.U., 1963. « Les produits verriers de Tmutarakani », *Keramika i steklo drevnej T. Moskwa*.
SINCLAIR, G.E., 1939. « A method of beadmaking in Ashanti », *Man*, 1939, n° 111.
SLEEN, W.G.N. VAN DER, 1956. « Trade-wind beads », *Man*, n° 27.
SLEEN, W.G.N. VAN DER, 1958. « Ancient glass beads of East and Central Africa and the Indian Ocean », *J. Roy. Anthr. Inst.*, vol. 88, pt. II, pp. 203-216, ill.
SLEEN, W.G.N. VAN DER, 1960.« De kralen van Riebeeck en anderen », *Westerheem*, t. IX, n° 9-10, pp. 110-111, pl. 8.
SLEEN, W.G.N. VAN DER, 1960. « Les collection Malgaches du Musée de Nîmes (France) », *Le Naturaliste Malgache*, vol. XII, pp. 184-191, ill.
SLEEN, W.G.N. VAN DER, 1961. « De wetenschap van de asbelt », *Panorama*.
SLEEN, W.G.N. VAN DER, 1962. *Glaskralen*, Bussum, 44 pp., 38 fig.
SLEEN, W.G.N. VAN DER, 1962. « The production of «antique» beads in Amsterdam in the 17th century », *Annales du 2ᵉ Congrès des Journées Internationales du Verre à Leyde, Hollande*.
SLEEN, W.G.N. VAN DER, 1963. « Trade-wind beads once more », *Man*, n° 154, pp. 128-129.
SLEEN, W.G.N. VAN DER, 1963. « A bead factory in Amsterdam in the 17th century », *Man*, n° 218-239, pp. 172-174.
SLEEN, W.G.N. VAN DER, 1963. « Beadmaking in 17th century Amsterdam », *Archaeology*, vol. 16, n° 4, pp. 260-263.
SLEEN, W.G.N. VAN DER, 1964. « Kralenfabricatie in Amsterdam in de 17de eeuw », *Ons Amsterdam*, vol. 16, n° 8.
SLOMANN, W., 1959. « Saetrangfunnet », *Norske Oldfun. Univ. Oldsaks* (Oslo).
SOLOVIEV, G.F. and KROPOTKIN, V.V., 1953. « On the production, distribution, and chronology of glass bracelets in ancient Russia », in *Brief Reports of I.I.M.K.*, n° 49, pp. 21-25.

Sordinas, A., 1965. « Report on the manufacture and marketing of the Adjagba beads in Ghana », *Journal of Glass Studies*, vol. VII, 1965, pp. 114-119, ill.
Stanley, H.E.J., 1866. *A Description of the Coast of East Africa by Duarte Barbosa, a Portuguese, 16th Century* (Hakluyt Soc., vol. 35).
Stoll, J., 1939. *Die Alemannen in Haifingen, Württemberg* (Germ. Denkm. der Frühzeit, Band 4).
Stone, J.F.S., and Thomas, L.C., 1956. « The use and distribution of faience », *Proc. Prehist. Society*, vol. XXII.
Strohl, A., 1954. « Die Reihengräber der Karlovingischen Zeit im Oberpfalz », *Materialhefte zur Bayer. Vorgeschichte* (München).
Theal, G.M., 1898. *Records of South-eastern Africa*, vol. II.
Thierry, Solange Bernard, 1960. *Perles Magiques de Madagascar* (Société des Africanistes, Tananarive).
Thierry, Solange Bernard, 1961. « Inventaire des perles de fouilles à Madagascar », *Bulletin de l'Académie Malgache*, nouv. série, 37.
Tornati, Maria, and van der Sleen, W.G.N., 1960. « L'analisi chimica aiuta l'archaeologia », *Vetro e silicati*, vol. IV, n° 23, pp. 19-24, ill.
Ugrelidza, N.N., 1961. *Verre de la vieille Georgia* (Tbilisi).
Vaillant, F. le, 1803. *Second voyage dans l'intérieur de l'Afrique* (Paris).
Veeck, K., 1931. *Alemannengräber in Württemberg* (Germ. Denkm. Frühzeit, Berlin).
Villiers, A. 1934. *The Sons of Sindbad* (London).
Wales, H.G. Quaritsch, 1937. *Towards Angkor* (London).
Werner, J., 1935. *Münzdatierte Austrasische Grabfunde* (Germ. Denkm. Frühzeit, Berlin).
Werner, J., 1953. « Das Alemannen Gräberfeld von Bulach », *Monogr. zur Urgeschichte der Schweiz*, Bd. 9 (Basel).
Wheeler, R.E. Mortimer, 1946. « Arikamedu », *Ancient India*, vol. 2.
Wheeler, R.E. Mortimer, 1948. « The Brahmapuri and Chandravalli excavations », *Ancient India*, vol. 4.
Wheeler, Sir R.E. Mortimer, 1953. *The Cambridge History of India*, suppl. vol., *The Indus Civilization* (Cambridge).
Wheeler, Sir R.E. Mortimer, 1954. *Rome Beyond the Imperial Frontiers* (London).
Wikar, H.J., 1799. *The Journal of H.J. Wikar* (V. Riebeeck Soc., vol. XV, Capetown).
Wild, R.P., 1937. « A method of beadmaking in the Gold Coast », *Man*, n° 115.
Woodward, A., 1959 and 1960. « Indian trade goods. Glass beads. Screenings », *The Oregon Archeol. Soc.*, vols. 8 & 9, n° 3.
Woodward, A., 1965. « Indian trade goods », *Oregon Archeol. Soc.*, pp. 4-17.
Woolley, Sir C. Leonard, 1954. *Excavations at Ur*.
Zeiss, H., 1945. *Grabfunde aus dem Spanischen West Gothen Reich* (Germ. Denkm. der Völkerwanderungszeit, Berlin).
Zurn, H., 1956. « Die vorgesch. Funde in Dettingen », *Veröff. Staatl. Anst.* Heft 3 (Stuttgart).

Index

A

aborigines, 27.
aboriginal, 116.
Aden, 77.
Adriatic, 63.
Afrasiab, 59.
Africa, 38, 49, 73, 84, 116.
   central, 85, 92, 114.
   east, 56, 76, 85.
   north, 85.
   south, 56, 83.
   west, 49, 103, 116.
agate, 17, 56, 70, 96.
aggry bead, 49.
air-bubbles, 19, 25, 81.
Akhenaten, 21.
Aleppo, 58.
Alexandria, 63.
alkali, 19, 22, 59, 70.
Allahabad, 12, 73.
d'Almeida, 88.
amazonite, 61, 70.
ambassador bead, 38, 85.
amber, 38, 55, 79.
Ameland, 112.
Amenophis, 21.
America
   central, 119.
   north, 117.
   south, 119.
amethyst, 17, 57, 74, 97.
Amlash, 70.
Amman, 50, 67.
Amsterdam, 38, 65, 98, 108.
amulet, 48.
Anaconda mines, 119.
analyses, 93, 100.
Anatolia, 58, 67.
ancient beads, 75, 87.
Andhra period, 81.
Angkor, 97.
Angola, 83.
annular, 85, 91.
Aquileia, 16, 48, 63, 107.
arabesque bead, 49.
Arabian, 76.
Arabs, 77, 82, 90.
archaeological congress, 21.
Arikamedu, 76, 94.
Arkell, Dr. A.J., 55.
Armenia, 21, 59.
Asia, 49.
Assyria, 21.
Atjeh, 96.
aventurine, 113.
Ayuthia, 97.
Azerbaijan, 21, 59.

B

Baal Hammon, 65.
Babylonia, 21, 77.
Bagamoyo, 92.
Bahmani period, 75.
baked bead, 27, 114.
Bali, 99, 108.
Baltic, 105.
Bantu, 87.
baptismal font, 116.
Barcelona, 67.
barrel, 23, 35.
barros miudas, 82.
batik, 69.
bauxite, 116.
Bavaria, 114.
bead garden, 112.
bead of the water, 83.
beadcutter, 56.
beadwork, 85.
Bechuanaland, 87.
Beck, H.C., 16, 51, 72, 97.
Bedouin, 48.
Benin, Nigeria, 117.
beryl, 74.
Bezborodov, M.A., 21, 59.
bicone, 26, 38, 74, 89.
biconical, 69, 87.
Birmingham, 85.
black beads, 97, 107.
Black Sea, 59.
bloedkoraal, 56.
blow-torch, 23.
blown beads, 26.
Bobrova, O., 59.
Bohemia, 114.
Bombay, 79.
bone beads, 73, 116.
boring, 17.
Brahmapuri, 79.
brass, 83.
Brazil, 56.
Brenner, 105.
Briare, 87, 115.
bronze, 90.
Bushmen, 61, 87, 116.
Bussum, 110.
button beads, 70, 118.
Byzantine, 64.
Byzantium, 77, 113.

C

Cairo, 59, 103.
calcite, 56.
Calcutta, 12, 73.
Cambay, 18, 55, 69, 96.
Cambridge, England, 76.
Canaanite, 65.
Canada, 117.
cane bead, 26, 88.
Cape, 95.
capped bead, 49.
Captain Cook, 38.
carbon 14, 58.
Carthage, 65.
Caton Thomson, G., 84, 92.
Caucasus, 59.
cave, 84.
Celebes, 87.
Cevennes, 55.
Chad lake, 69, 103.
Chalcedony, 56.
Chenopodia, 59.
chequer bead, 47, 64.
chevron bead, 26, 46, 64.
chief, 84.
Chile, 119.
chimanda, 87.
China, 77, 102.
china, 76.
Chmielovska, A., 73.
chrome, 79.
classification, 51.
clay, 19, 27, 62.
cobalt, 22, 79.
coin, 71, 76.
collared bead, 38, 70.
Cologne, 64.
colour guide, 50.
coloured bead, 50.
combed bead, 46, 64.
Congo, 85.
copper, 22, 75, 113.
coral (red), 56.
core, 17, 61, 74.
« cornalijnen kralen », 56.
« cornaline d'Aleppo », 85.
cornelian, 17, 55, 69, 79, 89.
cornelian beads, 49, 56, 61.
cornerless cube, 58, 74.
costume jewelry, 114.
cotton, 92.
crucible, 22.
crumb bead, 46, 62.
crystal, 57.
cube, 23.
cult of the dead, 62.
cuprous oxide, 82.
cylinder, 23, 56, 61, 82.
cylinder bead, 70, 83, 115.
cylindrical, 17, 25, 67, 84.
Cyprus, 58.
Czechoslovakia, 114.

D

Dakar, 49.
Damascus, 9, 58, 67.
Danube, 105.
Dar es Salaam, 78, 84.
Deir el Bahari, 116.
Dekovna, M., 59.
Deopik, V.B., 59.
diameter, 28.
diaphanous, 71.
Dikshit, M.G., 73, 92.
diorite, 70.
disc beads, 61, 87, 118.
discoid, 79.
dot and ring, 70.
Dravidian, 77.
drawn beads, 23, 42, 75, 81.
drilled, 17.
drop-pendant, 69.
dust (golden), 26.
Dutch, 29, 69, 83.
Dutch beads, 89, 108.
Dutch East India Cy, 69, 100.
Dutch West India Cy, 110.
dynasties, 18th, 22nd, 19.

E

earthenware, 17, 22, 82.
Ecuador, 119.
Egypt, 12, 21, 48, 56, 61, 70, 81
Egyptian, 26, 48, 61, 77.
Eisen, 29.
ellipsoid, 26.
emerald, 74.
Encyclopaedia Britannica, 11.
England, 55.
English, 29, 85.
equator, 84.

etched beads, 49, 69, 74.
Etruscan, 64.
Europe, 48, 56, 69, 82.
  western, 55, 82.
European, 38, 56, 64, 79, 81, 114.
excavation, 76, 81.
eye beads, 42, 63, 71, 115.

F

fabrication, 19, 26.
faceted beads, 38.
faience, 17, 27, 50, 70.
fashion, 87.
feather type, 47.
felspar, 61, 70, 114.
fern type, 70.
Fingerlin, G., 112.
Flanders, 83.
Flinders Petrie, 21, 62.
Flores, 98, 108.
folded beads, 26, 74.
Fouché, 116.
Fourneau, 89.
France, 114.
Fremersdorf, F., 122.
French, 29.
French School of the
  Extrême-Orient, 97.
frit, 17, 61, 70.
funnel, 25.
furnace, 23.

G

Gablonz, 87, 114.
Gardafui, 77.
garden-roller beads, 116.
Gardner, G.S., 122.
garnet, 17, 57, 70.
Gasparetto, A., 113.
geometrical, 87.
Georgia, 21, 59.
German, 29.
Germany, 56.
Ghana, 103, 116.
glass, 19.
glass-jewelry, 42.
glass-makers, 21.
glaze, 17, 61.
Glazema, P., 122.
globular, 17, 23, 56, 81.
gold, 74, 83.
gold beads, 119.
gold-coloured, 42.
gold foil, 113.
gold-leaf beads, 25.
gold mines, 92.
gold stone, 113.
Good Hope, Cape of, 83.
Gottardi, Dr. V., 12.
granite, 70.
granulated, 62.
s'Graveland, 108.
Greek, 77.
Grimaldi man, 55.
guide-bead, 79.
Gujerat, 18, 56, 69, 95.

H

hand-perforated beads, 26, 74.
Hanno, 3, 111.
Harden, D.B., 10.
Hebron, 48, 63, 115.
Heekeren, H.R. van, 72, 99.
Hensel, W., 59.
Herzogenrath, 87.
hexagonal, 26, 38, 85.
Hippalos, 77.
Hittites, 19.
hoard, 84.
Holland, 89, 98.
hollow, 26.
home-industry, 27.
Hoop, J. van der, 82.
horned beads, 48, 71.
Hottentot, 83.
Hruby, V., 123.
Hudig, F.W., 108.
Hudson Bay Cy, 118.
human-head beads, 67.

I

Ibiza, 67.
Ibn Batuta, 88.
imitation, 108.
India, 12, 26, 55, 70, 82.
Indian Ocean, 12, 56, 83.

Indian red, 75, 82.
Indians, 77,
  American, 55.
  Canadian, 111.
  Totem, 118.
Indonesia, 56, 98.
initiation, 116.
inscription 76
iron, 22, 79, 113.
Israël, 48.
Italian, 29, 42.
Italy, 67.
ivory, 83, 116.
Ivory Coast, 116.

Jablonec, see Gablonz.
Jaipur, 12.
Japan, 76, 99.
jasper, 70, 97, 116.
Java, 12, 72, 83, 90.
Jericho, 58, 118.
Jerusalem, 59, 67.
jet, 55.
Johore, 82, 97.
Jordan, 48, 56.

K

Kalahari desert, 116.
Kano, 69, 117.
Kaufbueren, 114.
Kausambi, 94.
Kenya, 82.
Khami, 84.
Kilwa, 78, 82, 116.
Kirkman, J.S., 79, 82.
Kisa, A., 123.
Kolhapur, 79.
« Korallenslijper », 55.
« kraal », 55.
Krakov, 59.
Krumphanzlova, 59.
Kruzwicka, 59.

L

Lamu, 88.
lapis lazuli, 17, 58, 70.
lead, 19, 99.
lead glass, 59, 100.
lenticular beads, 38, 79.
Leyden, 90.
lime, 19, 61, 70.
Limes, 64.
limestone, 70, 88, 116.
Limpopo, 83.
Livingstone, 44, 85.
London, 76.
love letters, 87.
lozenge, 89.
Luango, 83.
lustre, 114.
Lwowa, Z.A., 59.

M

Madagascar, 12, 56, 90.
magic, 90.
Malacca, 56.
Malagasy, 90.
malay, 90.
Malaya, 96.
Malgaches, 88.
Malindi, 78.
Malleret, L., 97.
Mameluke bead, 72.
manganese, 22, 69.
Mapungubwe, 81, 116.
marl, 19.
mart, 76, 95.
marver, 25, 42, 103.
Masingo, 11.
Matabele, 85.
Mathew, Rev. Dr. G., 88.
Matopo Hills, 85.
matrix, 47, 71.
medicine bottle, 90, 116.
Mediterranean, 48, 64, 81.
Mekong river, 97.
melon beads, 23, 62, 97.
Menes, 61.
Merovingian beads, 64.
Mesopotamia, 17, 58, 73, 116.
microalin, 61, 70.
microscope, 82.
migration, 79.
millefiori beads, 47, 103.
Millot, J., 88.
mirrors, 90.
modern beads, 113.
Mogadishu, 88.
Moluccas, 87.
Monomotapa, 92.
monopoly, 113.
monsoon, 77.
mosaic, 59, 113.
mosaic beads, 47, 103.
mould, 23.
moulded beads, 26, 38, 74.
mpande, 87.
multifaceted beads, 56.
multiple-wound beads, 23, 74, 81, 97.
mummy-net bead, 19, 61, 97.
Murano, 12, 81, 113.
museum, 115.
    Allahabad, 96.
    Aquileia, 107.
    Brussels, Tervueren, 114.
    Bulawayo, 84.
    Cairo, 67.
    Calcutta, 96.
    Cambridge, 76.
    Djakarta, 99.
    Holland, Leeuwarden, Frisian, 112.
    Weert, Mission, 99.
    Japan, Shosoin, 102.
    Tokyo, Ueno, 76.
    London, British Museum, 113.
    Nimes, France, 90.
    Oxford, Ashmolean, 76, 62.
    Paris, Cernuchi, 99.
    Peking, 101.
    Rome, Italy, Terme, 63.
    Singapore, Raffles, 97.
    Tunis, Bardo, 67.
    Lavigerie (Carthage), 65, 102.
muti sala beads, 98.

N

Napoleon, 48.
Narmer, 61.
Natal, 56.
natron, 69.
ndoro, 87.
neolithic, 58.
Neri, A., 23.
New Empire, Egypt, 62.
Nicosia, 58.
Nigeria, 116.
Nile, 77.
Nîmes, 89.
nitre, 19.
Nyasa Lake, 82.

O

Oberstein, 56.
oblate, 25, 38, 62, 71.
Oc-èo, 97.
ogee bead, 46.
ogee pattern, 70.
onyx, 19, 57, 70.
opaque, 12, 29, 73, 81.
Opole, Poland, 59.
Opone, 77.
Orange River, 83.
Orient, 63, 108.
oriental, 64.
ox-eye beads, 84.
Oxford, 76.

P

Pakistan, 38, 78.
Palestine, 65, 101.
palm-leaf bead, 47.
palm-oil, 85.
Papuans, 55.
Pasquato, M., 48, 113.
paste, 29, 61, 88.
payment, 25.
pearl (false). 26.
Pemba, 79.
pendant, 85.
Pengalonga, 84.
pentagon beads, 38, 99.
Perak, 82.
perforation, 17, 23, 38, 61, 85.
perimeter, 28.
Periplus, 77, 97.
permanganate, 73, 113.
Persia, 67, 73.
Persian, 71, 81.
Pharaoh, 21.
Pharaonic, 61.
Phœnician, 65, 105.
pincer, 23.
plastic, 114.
Poland, 59.
Polish, 29.
Pompeii, 49, 63.
Pondichery, 76, 96.
porcelain beads, 17, 26, 114.
porcupine, 55.
porphyry, 70.
Portuguese, 78, 81, 88, 91.
potash, 19, 101.
potsherd, 71.
pottery, 73, 82.
pound beads, 25.
Pratt, P.P., 110.
predynastic Egypt, 61, 62.
prehistoric beads, 55.
pre-mosque beads, 88.
pressed beads, 26, 114.
prism, 23.
Ptolemy, 17, 62.
pulverized, 27.
Punic, 67.
Punt, 77.
Purdalpur, 75.

Q

quartz, 18, 56, 61, 74, 97.
Quaritsch Wales, 97.

R

Read, H., 111.
red-capped beads, 49.
red coral, 56.
red-on-green beads, 84, 91.
red-on-white beads, 84.
Red Sea, 76.
reticulated beads, 70.
Rhine, 61, 79, 105.
Rhodesia, 11, 84, 92.
Rhône, 105.
Riebeeck, J. van, 83.
ring beads, 61.
ringlets, 62, 70.
rock-crystal, 63.
rock-shelter, 84.
rod, 23, 81, 113.
Römisch-Germanische Kommission, 107.
Roman, 25, 63, 71, 111.
Roman Empire, 63.
Romano-Egyptian, 63, 98.
Rome, Italy, 63, 77.
rosary, 114.
rosette beads, 26.
Rouffaer, G.P., 98.
ruby, 74.
ruin-beads, 12.

S

Sahara, 69.
St. Eustatius island, 110.
St. Mark's, Venice, 113.
Samarkand, 59, 113.
sample-book, 113.
sand, 70.
Sankalia, 79.
Satavahana period, 81.
scallop beads, 46.
Scheherazade, 78.
seed-bead, 117.
segmented beads, 62.
selenium, 75.
Selukwe, 84.
semi-precious, 18, 58, 73.
shell, 70, 85, 92.
shell beads, 87.
    Abalone (haliotis), 118.
    Achatina sp., 87, 116.
    clam, 118.
    Conus, 87, 116.
    Dentalium, elephant tooth shell, 58, /118.
ostrich-egg, 87, 116.
Tridacna gigas, 87, 116.
Turritella, 26.
Unio sp., 87.
Sindbad, 78.
slave-trader, 85.
slaves, 83.
Slavia Antiqua, 21.
soda, 19, 61, 70, 108.
Sofala, 78, 91.
Sokotra, 77.
Solutréan cave, 55.
Somalia, 77.
spacing beads, 42.
spherical beads, 51, 75.
spirally-wound beads, 71, 83.
spotted beads, 42.
square beads, 26, 70, 89, 115.
standard beads, 11.
Stanley, 49, 82.
star beads, 26, 89, 111.
State Archives, The Hague, 56.
Staz. Sper. del Vetro, Murano, 93.
steatite, 79.
stone beads, 17, 73.
stratified beads, 67.
striped beads, 25, 46, 64, 117.
Sumatra, 78, 96.
Sumerian, 49, 87.
Sun-God, 21.
Syria, 48, 64, 113.
Syrian beads, 48, 107.

T

tabular beads, 19, 26.
Taj Mahal, 49.
Tananarive, 89.
Tanga, 78.
Tanzania, 82.
Tashkent, 21, 59.
technique, 22.
Teheran, 69.
Tel Aviv, 63.
Tell el Amarna, 2, 48, 81.
Tete, 83.
Thebes, Egypt, 21.
Timurlane, 59.
Tokyo, 82.
tomb, 76, 88.
Tornati, M., 12, 93.
trade-route, 51, 112.
trade-wind beads, 12, 77, 116.
traina beads, 85.
transparent, 17, 82.
Transvaal, 81, 116.
trigonal, 26, 70.
tube, 19, 25, 81, 113.
tubular, 70, 83.
Tunisia, 65.
turquoise, 70.
Tutankhamun, 61.
Tyre, 65.

U

Uganda, 87.
Ugrelidza, Mrs, 21.
Ur, 58, 87.
U.S.A., 85.
U.S.S.R., 21.

V

Vasco da Gama, 85.
Venda, 83.
Venetian beads, 42, 85, 113.
Venice, 23, 40, 59, 81.
Victoria Falls, 85.
Vohémar, 89.

W

Wampum beads, 118.
Warsaw, 21.
wax, 69, 73.
Wheeler, Sir Mortimer, 96.
wire, 23.
witch-doctor, 85.
Woolley, Sir Leonard, 58.
wound beads, 23, 42, 81.
Wroclaw, 59.

Y

Ypey, J., 122.

Z

Zambesi, 83.
Zambia, 84.
Zanzibar, 12, 73, 81.
Zimbabwe, 12, 79, 92.
zoned bead, 46, 67.
Zoutpansbergen, 83.